# SpringerBriefs in Education

## Key Thinkers in Education

**Series editor**

Paul Gibbs, London, UK

This briefs series publishes compact (50 to 125 pages) refereed monographs under the editorial supervision of the Advisory Editor, Professor Paul Gibbs, Middlesex University, Nicosia, Cyprus. Each volume in the series provides a concise introduction to the life and work of a key thinker in education and allows readers to get acquainted with their major contributions to educational theory and/or practice in a fast and easy way.

More information about this series at http://www.springer.com/series/10197

Michael A. Peters · Jeff Stickney

# Wittgenstein's Education: 'A Picture Held Us Captive'

Springer

Michael A. Peters
Faculty of Education
Wilf Malcolm Institute of Educational Research
The University of Waikato
Hamilton, Waikato
New Zealand

Jeff Stickney
Ontario Institute for Studies in Education
University of Toronto
Toronto, ON
Canada

ISSN 2211-1921 ISSN 2211-193X (electronic)
SpringerBriefs in Education
ISSN 2211-937X ISSN 2211-9388 (electronic)
SpringerBriefs on Key Thinkers in Education
ISBN 978-981-10-8410-2 ISBN 978-981-10-8411-9 (eBook)
https://doi.org/10.1007/978-981-10-8411-9

Library of Congress Control Number: 2018931507



This Springer imprint is published by the registered company Springer Nature Singapore Pte Ltd. part of Springer Nature
The registered company address is: 152 Beach Road, #21-01/04 Gateway East, Singapore 189721, Singapore

Portrait of Ludwig Wittgenstein by Karen Duplisea (oil on linen panel, commissioned 2017; original photograph by Moritz Nähr, d. 1945)

# Preface

Upon completion of a larger Springer project, a co-edited volume of 50 chapters from 45 authors in 14 countries entitled *A Companion to Wittgenstein on Education: Pedagogical Investigations* (2017), Peters and Stickney decided to co-author the present book for this series, *Springer Briefs in Education: Key Thinkers in Education*. We are grateful to Nick Melchior, Ang Lay Peng, Paul Gibbs, Balaji Sundarrajan and Albert Paap at Springer for their assistance throughout the process of writing of this book. Some of our colleagues may wonder: 'Why another book on Wittgenstein and education, at this time?' In the larger volume we included, among many renowned figures in the field of Wittgenstein scholarship in Philosophy of Education, around ten emerging scholars who had recently finished or were in the process of completing their doctoral dissertations. Having served on doctoral committees where the enigmatic figure of Wittgenstein was brought into play with issues in education, we saw the use in providing a short book that better helps to introduce Wittgenstein's later philosophy to colleagues within the broader academic community—not just within our narrower and more technical subfield of Philosophy of Education.

For anyone working with Wittgenstein's philosophy in education, it can be frustrating trying to convey the connection to committee members or colleagues who are experts in their own domains of research but are unfamiliar with Wittgenstein's thinking and its possible applications within education. It is our hope that the material here will also be of interest to practitioners within education, working either in educational administration or in teaching, as well as those entering the profession in teacher training institutes. Our featured philosopher, Ludwig Wittgenstein, attended the Teacher Training facility in Vienna (1918–1919) and later taught in rural Austria for 6 years (1920–1926). One of the questions we entertain is whether that makes his thinking more relevant to education, broadly speaking, without looking to him for a pedagogical creed or method.

Hamilton, New Zealand — Michael A. Peters
Toronto, Canada — Jeff Stickney

# Contents

# Abbreviations

| | |
|---|---|
| BB | Blue and Brown Books |
| BT | Big Typescript |
| CV | Culture and value |
| LC | Lectures and Conversations—(LA: Lecture on Aesthetics, in LC) |
| LE | Lecture on Ethics (in PO: Philosophical Occasions) |
| LFM | Lectures on the Foundations of Mathematics |
| LPP | Wittgenstein's Lectures on Philosophical Psychology 1946–47 |
| LW 1 or 2 | Last Writings on the Philosophy of Psychology |
| LRKM | Letters to Russell, Keynes and Moore |
| LWVC | Ludwig Wittgenstein and the Vienna Circle |
| N | Notebooks 1914–1916 |
| OC | On Certainty |
| PG | Philosophical Grammar |
| PI | Philosophical Investigations |
| PO | Philosophical Occasions |
| PR | Philosophical Remarks |
| RFGB | Remarks on Frazer's Golden Bough |
| RFM | Remarks on the Foundations of Mathematics |
| RPP 1 or 2 | Remarks on the Philosophy of Psychology |
| TLP | Tractatus Logico-philosophicus |
| WL | Wittgenstein's Lectures, Cambridge 1930–1932 |
| WN | Wittgenstein's Nachlass: The Bergen electronic edition |
| WV | Wörterbuch für Volksschulen |
| Z | Zettel |

# Chapter 1
# Picturing Wittgenstein's Relationships to Education

A picture held us captive. And we could not get outside it, for it lay in our language and language seemed to repeat it to us inexorably. (PI §115)

## 1.1 Introduction: Quick Studies (*etude*) for a Philosophical Portrait

Wittgenstein is widely considered to be one of the most important philosophers of the twentieth century, strongly influencing the directions of both analytic and post-analytical philosophy (Child 2011). Early in his studies at Cambridge, Bertrand Russell informed Wittgenstein's visiting sister, Hermine, that he expected the next great discovery in philosophy to come from her brother Ludwig. Austrian physicist Moritz Schlick mentioned in a letter to Einstein that he was reading Wittgenstein's *Tractatus* and subsequently arranged a meeting with Wittgenstein in 1927 through his sister Margarete (Oberdan 2013). Wittgenstein's work in the philosophy of logic, mathematics, mind and language established him as the one of the founders of two movements—logical empiricism (associated with the Vienna or 'Schlick Circle') and Oxford-style ordinary language analysis. Wittgenstein's work is difficult to read and there are many competing interpretations of his philosophy, but its impact has been felt in the arts, humanities and social sciences. In philosophy of education, following the 'revolution' in analytic philosophy, Wittgenstein inspired R. S. Peters' London school in the 1960s and 70s—focused on the clarification of concepts. During the 1980s and after, Wittgenstein's work, especially the *Philosophical Investigations* became the basis for a more sustained and varied treatment often following Stanley Cavell, Richard Rorty and Jean-Francois Lyotard: thinkers who provided interpretations that emphasized the figure of the child, anti-foundationalism and 'the postmodern condition'. These topics are still very much alive today in philosophy of education, although relatively few in the broad field of education read this specialized literature.



M. A. Peters and J. Stickney, *Wittgenstein's Education: 'A Picture Held Us Captive'*, SpringerBriefs on Key Thinkers in Education
https://doi.org/10.1007/978-981-10-8411-9_1

Addressing 'Wittgenstein's education' we open what is likely too large a topic for a short book, inviting a wide scope of commentary on his own learning processes in becoming an engineer, educator and philosopher, as well as his concepts of and contributions to education. With so much literature already in existence, what more can we possibly say about these topics? Drawing on earlier biographical treatments (see Bartley 1973; Monk 1991), we situate Wittgenstein's several relationships to education by focusing on later writings in which the reluctant Cambridge professor harkens back to his earlier experience as an elementary teacher in rural Austria. In this later work, we find the thinker sharing simple vignettes of teacher–pupil interactions as a heuristic device in his now famous but rather nebulous 'philosophical investigations' of language and meaning.

Our subtitle is drawn from Wittgenstein's remark in the *Philosophical Investigations* (§115): 'A picture held us captive. And we could not get outside it, for it lay in our language and language seemed to repeat it to us inexorably.'[1] Sometimes Wittgenstein speaks literally and aesthetically about pictures, such as how one might recognize a fake painting using very subtle cues (as almost 'imponderable evidence', PI, p. 228), or how well-off people from good schools who have travelled to the Louvre have a different kind of aesthetic appreciation (LC 9); at other times noting how we instantly recognize when a painting is hung improperly (e.g. different when upside-down, LC 35), or how only those immersed within a religious *form of life* (LC 58) might react strongly to a painting of (say) Mary with baby Jesus or God's All-seeing Eye and Judgement Day (LC 55, 71). This particular reflection on a 'captivating picture' in PI §115 is figurative, however, and applies foremost to images conveyed in his earlier work in the *Tractatus*: what is commonly called his 'picture-theory of language' in which meaning is secured by depicting things or states of affairs in the real world (see Burbules and Peters 2003).[2] His

[1]Following convention, titles for Wittgenstein's works are abbreviated (PI = Philosophical Investigations, RFM = Remarks on the Foundation of Mathematics, OC = On Certainty, WL = Wittgenstein's Lectures, CV = Culture Value, PO = Philosophical Occasions), with section (§) or page number (p.), with full citation and initials (e.g. RFM) in the References. See Abbreviation list, p. ii??

[2]Wittgenstein later reflects back on his picture-theory in the *Tractatus*, seeing such depiction as one of several ways of forming empirical propositions:

> If a proposition is conceived as a picture of the state of affairs it describes and a proposition is said to show just how things stand if it's true, and thus to show the possibility of the asserted state of affairs, still the most that the proposition can do is what a painting or relief does: and so it can at any rate not set forth what is just not the case. So it depends wholly on our grammar what will be called possible and what not, i.e., what that grammar permits. But surely that is arbitrary! Certainly; but the grammatical constructions we call empirical propositions (e.g., ones which describe a visible distribution of objects in space and could be replaced by a representational drawing) have a particular application, a particular use. (PG §82' cf. TLP 1.1–1.21)

Wittgenstein also had in mind such gripping images as the empiricist model of perception (OC §90), the cellophane picture of our separation from nature and god (CV 50e), and the Aquinas, inspiration model of calculating (PI §232–35).

ambitious philosophical task in the early *Tractatus*, associated with the school of thought known as *logical positivism,* was to show everything that could be meaningfully said and to pass over in silence what fell outside these parameters for sensible language. Wittgenstein turned his critique on this faulty 'picture': what he likened to seeking the 'crystalline purity of logic' (an ideal, imaginary world in which we find no real traction); in his later *Philosophical Investigations* he advocated instead acceptance of language-in-use, perfectly ordered and meaningful as it is ordinarily practiced on the 'rough ground' (PI §108). In other words, possibly a source of confusion for readers, the image of language being meaningful in so far as it accurately portrays the external world is one of the 'pictures' (he comes to observe) that we have inherited over time (e.g. from Augustine, PI §1) that still limits or distorts our thinking about how language actually works. In another analogy, he says it is like looking through a lens which distorts our vision, failing to realize that we could remove the spectacles (PI §103). Much of his philosophical teaching—the education he provided students at Cambridge and for readers of his later writing—is directed to freeing us from this kind of captivity, liberating us from misleading pictures or viewpoints that lay in our language as traps (see PO 185, in Ch 2). Instead of teaching us anything new or scientific, he says, his later project was to offer a clear description of the workings of language as we find it used, so as to avoid missteps occasioned by these deeply entrenched pictures.

Making interpretation a little more confusing, despite moving away from a picture-theory of meaning Wittgenstein persisted in his later philosophical remarks to talk about teaching or persuading others as conveying 'pictures'. Returning to aesthetic reactions, we learn techniques of 'picturing' the meaning or allusive imagery in a stanza of poetry (LC 4), 'drawing' connections that stand as a rule or practice for others to understand what we 'see' in the poem or painting (LC 68, 71–2). We can even convey a 'picture', he remarks, of what is called 'a very high culture', such as German music in the last two centuries, or in architecture when many people attend to details instead of accepting imitations (LC 7). Here is another, simple example applied to learning a mathematical proof (see Stickney 2017; Rider 2017; cf. Ch 3):

> You get him to decide on accepting this picture. And you do so by means of the proof, i.e. by exhibiting a series of pictures, or simply by shewing him the picture. What moves him to decide does not matter here. The main thing is that it is a question of accepting the picture. (RFM IV.12; cf. BB 89–90)

In another case also drawn from his later writing, 'pictures' are said to be provided in the proof of claims, pointing us in the direction of considering the ground of possibilities—the grammatical relations—we have for accepting some pictures as convincing and rejecting others.

> I should like you to say: "Yes, it's true, that can be imagined, that may even have happened!" But was I trying to draw your attention to the fact that you are able to imagine this? I wanted to put this picture before your eyes, and your *acceptance* of this picture consists in your being inclined to regard a given case differently; that is, to compare it with *this* series of pictures. I have changed your *way of seeing*. (I once read somewhere that a geometrical

> figure, with the words "Look at this", serves as a proof for certain Indian mathematicians. This looking too effects an alteration in one's way of seeing.) (Z §461; cf. PI §144)

Sometimes these shared pictures—such as our view that the earth is a sphere—may stretch over millennia and across many cultures, thus constituting a 'world picture' (*Weltbild*, see Ch 4), or undoubted 'bedrock' within our culture.

> We form *the picture* of the earth as a ball floating freely in space and not altering essentially in a hundred years. I said "We form the picture etc." and this picture now helps us in the judgment of various situations. ... (OC §146)
>
> The picture of the earth as a ball is a *good* picture, it proves itself everywhere, it is also a simple picture – in short, we work with it without doubting it. (OC §147)

Although this fact has been 'known' since the time of Pythagoras, Plato and Aristotle (6–5th c. B.C.), our secondary and even post-secondary students usually find it difficult to produce the evidence or reasons (the foundations for 'knowledge' as justified-true-belief) for adhering to this compelling picture: even though Eratosthenes was measuring the circumference of the spherical earth back in the Third century B.C. If a student denied the earth was sphere the teacher might be at a loss as to how to go on to instruct this pupil in other facts (see OC §§310–15), such as the very old age of the planet (over 4.5 billion years) and of the universe in which we find ourselves in today (around 13 billion years old).

> I can imagine a man who had grown up in quite special circumstances and been taught that the earth came into being 50 years ago, and therefore believed this. We might instruct him: the earth has long...etc.—We should be trying to give him our picture of the world (*Weltbild*).
>
> This would happen through a kind of *persuasion*. (OC §262)

The obscurity of Wittgenstein's often brief, frequently dialogical, and only occasionally sequential remarks is potentially lifted by reading many others, taking the meaning of each use of the word 'picture' from the particular context provided. With more familiarity, one gradually gains a sense of when Wittgenstein is actually making a philosophical claim and when he is expressing the views of an interlocutor (perhaps sounding the conventional position as a retort) or even talking to himself (as he often did on his long walks or as asides in the course of his teaching). The many quotes from Wittgenstein's corpus provided in this book are intended to help the reader gain some oversight on the major themes running through his philosophical work, as well as their connections to education, with the hope that 'light dawns gradually over the whole' (OC §141).

Throughout this book, we look at several cases of 'captivity within pictures', such as being bound to causal points of view.

> The insidious thing about the causal point of view is that it leads us to say: "Of course, it had to happen like that." Whereas we ought to think: it may have happened like that – and also in many other ways. (CV 37e)

Not only a problem in social sciences like psychology, this picture sometimes enters into the way authors discuss Wittgenstein's development as a thinker, or in how we talk about learning processes. In this chapter and in the next, we look at faulty pictures as a kind of foil, adding some polemical controversy to our narrative. In Chap. 2, for instance, we try to dispel confusion stemming from references in his later philosophy to 'training', a problem of interpretation that arises within the field of education when readers mistakenly think Wittgenstein is advocating forms of conditioning *as* his pedagogy, or as his view of education more generally. Instead of being able to pinpoint or verify the cause(s), or provide elaborate reasons for learning (e.g. rules), Wittgenstein points to the method of training as showing us the path by which a pupil comes to *master a technique* (e.g. practices as simple as the multiplication table, or using the word 'death' in contemplating 'eternal life', LC 71–2) or in coming to hold a concept with certainty, *as* true.

> ...What is the criterion for the way the formula is meant? Presumably the way we always use it, the way we were taught to use it. (RFM 1.1–2)

The normative aspect of training into regular ways of 'carrying-on' or 'going-on' has also led some to mistake Wittgenstein as being conservative, whereas we would note that his later philosophy and *On Certainty* in particular helps us understand how concepts and practices become deeply rooted (*bedrock and world pictures*) within a culture, making it difficult but not impossible for language users and practitioners to open them to critical inspection or revaluation (see Ch 4). Such caricatures of Wittgenstein—as a severe animal-trainer and conservative—do disservice both to Philosophy and to the many philosophers of education who have made productive use of his thinking to see anew several aspects of education.

Supporting this project is a portrayal of Wittgenstein, now familiar to philosophers of education, as a 'pedagogical philosopher' instead of a theorist of education (see Ch 3): a theme Michael Peters entertained when he was at the University of Illinois, taking hold soon after he had investigated the 'pedagogical turn' of Wittgenstein's life and writings. Addressing the pedagogical turn in Wittgenstein's writing, and seeing his later 'philosophy as pedagogy', became the basis of an interpretation shared with James Marshall, Nicholas Burbules and Paul Smeyers over the course of several publications (Peters and Marshall 1999; Peters et al. 2008). The now familiar trope (in philosophy of education) provides room to contest older interpretations, such as Wittgenstein's uptake within the analytic tradition as a mere surveyor of ordinary language usage (e.g. mapping the 'teaching' and 'learning' concepts), and to contemplate new connections with Continental philosophy and culture. Because this reading of Wittgenstein can be found in several other texts, we simply gloss over it here in the Introduction in order to provide readers new to this literature with sufficient background.

## 1.2 A Place for Biography: Significance Without Explanatory Force

Ludwig Josef Johann Wittgenstein (b.1889–d.1951) was born into a wealthy Viennese family, the youngest of eight children. The Wittgenstein children were first tutored at home, including governesses who spoke and taught different languages. Johannes Brahms was their music instructor. Ludwig's older brother Hans was a child prodigy, and Paul became a concert pianist for whom Ravel and others wrote concertos. Ludwig could whistle entire concertos (e.g. Schumann). *Palais Wittgenstein* was often visited by composers like Maurice Ravel and Richard Strauss, and Gustav Klimt was commissioned to paint the wedding portrait for Ludwig's sister Margarete.[3] Leaving behind this rich cultural milieu that no doubt informed his aesthetic appreciation, Wittgenstein came to Manchester in 1911 to study engineering. After reading Gottlob Frege's work on mathematics and logic, he went to Cambridge and initially audited Bertrand Russell's lectures on formal logic. He finally turned up at Russell's rooms at Nevile's Court, Trinity College to introduce himself on the 18th of October 1911, insisting on speaking in English (although Russell would often refer to him as 'my German'). In a now famous meeting, Wittgenstein asked Russell if he should pursue philosophy or return to aeronautics, depending on whether he was found to be a 'complete idiot'. 'Write me something', Russell said,[4] and after producing a commentary on Russell's own paper Wittgenstein was accepted into a prestigious academic circle.

Wittgenstein was admitted to the Moral Sciences Club on the 1st February 1912 as an undergraduate with the mathematician James Glaisher as his tutor and the logician William Johnson as his supervisor. He attended lectures by G. E. Moore, G. H. Hardy, J. E. Littlewood and Alfred North Whitehead. His friendship with both Moore and Russell deepened during this time. He met Lytton Strachey, and David Pinsent who was later to become his lover, and he moved in circles that included John Maynard Keynes, C. K. Ogden and Ferenc Békássy. Wittgenstein participated fully in the life of the college, also joining and trying to dominate discussion at the Apostles' Club. He attended Russell's lectures on the foundation of mathematics and Moore's lectures on psychology: themes that would occupy his philosophical thinking (and therefore titles of his posthumously published text) until his life was cut short by cancer in 1951. *Wittgenstein's Education,* however, does not merely linger on the modes of learning and teaching by which, or in spite of which, this enigmatic figure emerged as one of the most famous thinkers of the twentieth century, inspiring numerous commentaries on his life and a plethora of scholarly elucidations of his original movements of thought.

In many previous studies (especially within academic Philosophy), the question of education was seen as peripheral or incidental to Wittgenstein's philosophy—a

---

[3]Ludwig would later be the architect on sister Margarete's house.

[4]Russell's own account can be listened to on a recording: https://www.youtube.com/watch?v=cFXWKEc84ew.

kind of interregnum between two distinct philosophical periods in Wittgenstein's life: the *Tractatus* (the early Wittgenstein), and the *Philosophical Investigations* (late Wittgenstein).[5] Meredith Williams, Jose Medina, Beth Savickey, Michael Luntley, David Bakhurst and Stanley Cavell are notable exceptions within academic Philosophy for bringing education into the conversation. In this monograph, we argue for the centrality of education to Wittgenstein's life and works without extending it explanatory force. This educational background informs or nuances how we read his many 'scenes of instruction', as Cavell (1979) refers to them, without reducing the meaning or significance of these philosophical vignettes to their origins in his life: moments in his personal history captured in the many biographies. To put this most simply, and in keeping with Wittgenstein's later philosophy: his philosophical writing has to be read in context, and this educational milieu is part of the broader context or background that culturally surrounds and to some extent intellectually grounds his thinking. Central to this interpretation is the 7 years he spent training and as an elementary teacher. Rather than viewing 'education' and 'teaching' as insignificant episodes confined to this period we argue (with Savickey, Medina and others; see Ch 3) that Wittgenstein's relationship to education—his own education, his experience as an elementary and then university teacher—were of central significance to both the man and his philosophy.

In raising our reader's expectations, it is sometimes necessary to then deflate them. What can we *really* glean from the few facts we have about Wittgenstein's education (see Monk 1990, 14–16)? A brief synopsis of his educational background reveals significant details woven together in the tapestry of his life (see Z §§567–69, Ch 2), none of which on their own explain how he emerged as a prominent philosopher. After homeschooling, he attended *Realschule* in Linz (1903–06),[6] pursuing an applied or technical education instead of an academic (gymnasium) programme like his older sisters. He was not very happy or successful at school (i.e. relatively low grades and serious dissatisfaction with school life). He tended to do better in the humanities and in religious studies in particular. He stuttered and other boys made fun of him (and he, them). He attended a technical high school in Berlin for three semesters studying mechanical engineering and later began a Ph.D. at the Victoria University of Manchester in 1908 before changing direction entirely in 1911: following his interest in the foundations of mathematics by visiting Gottlob Frege and then auditing Bertrand Russell's lectures on *Principia Mathematica* and logic before committing to study philosophy with Bertrand Russell and G. E. Moore at Cambridge. He wanted to abandon his studies at Cambridge and move to Russia, but although he and his companion Skinner studied Russian and travelled there in 1935 he was eventually counselled against this move by G. E. Moore and John Maynard Keynes. Although he was one of the wealthiest men in Europe, he

[5]Danièle Moyal-Sharrock (2004) would say that his later works such as *On Certainty* and *Last Writings on the Philosophy of Psychology* amount to a third iteration of his philosophical thinking.

[6]Adolf Hitler attended the same school at this time also, but there is no indication of any contact (Monk 1990, 15). Wittgenstein was ahead of his class by one year, and Hitler behind one year.

gave away his fortune in support of artists and in securing the livelihoods of his siblings. Not much light is cast, we presume, from these biographical details on their own. Although his life makes an interesting story (even for those unfamiliar with his philosophy), this kind of report is tangential to our project.

Being mindful of his life and times is central to the way we receive Wittgenstein's often fragmentary and aphoristic writings, most of which were published posthumously and were edited and translated by his colleagues or students such as Elizabeth Anscombe and G. W. von Wright. Interpretation requires deep contextualization, including sketches of the cultural and historical milieu in which he laboured. Here *Wittgenstein's Education* takes on another meaning: the sense in which he educated *us* in our thinking about philosophy of language and mind, but also—rather inadvertently or unintentionally—about education itself. In this light, his experiences as a learner and teacher are not paramount, but are certainly relevant background in setting the stage for the ways in which we think alongside or with Wittgenstein. Ray Monk's (1990/1991) insightful biography reopened inquiry into Wittgenstein's experience as a teacher, using letters to and from such familiars as Bertrand Russell, Maurice O'Connor Drury and his sister Hermine Wittgenstein to bring a fresh perspective to earlier biographical accounts by William Bartley (1973). Most authoritatively, Beth Savickey (1999, 2017) has produced detailed background on Wittgenstein's training and experience as an elementary teacher in rural Austria, and has carefully considered at least four possible lines of reasoning as to how this may have influenced his later style of teaching and philosophical thinking and writing at Cambridge. Building on their excellent work, we are nevertheless cautious about extracting from Wittgenstein's biography, whether from his own education or from his teaching experience, hints at causes behind the 'production of genius' or clues as to how one should teach. Not only are such causal and normative accounts too simplistic, they indicate a search for theories of learning or of psychological development Wittgenstein would have abhorred (see PI §109 below).

It is easy for authors to slip into this speculative mode of thinking, as it is for readers to be seduced by its charm into thinking that a satisfactory explanation has been delivered. Hamilton, for instance, astutely notes that Wittgenstein's writing style is highly practical (case-oriented) and pictorial (using models and diagrammatic sketches), but then goes beyond description in wondering if his technical training in engineering was similar in influence to his philosophical writing, as was Einstein's work in the patent office instrumental in his work on theoretical physics (relativity).[7] More specifically, Hamilton (2001, 53–54) argues that 'Wittgenstein's practice as a design engineer informed his conception of the *Bild* theory of language in the *Tractatus,* and that understanding the character of his scientific training gives us deeper insight on doctrine of what can only be shown and not said.' Although it is interesting to speculate what kinds of changes took place in Wittgenstein's mind

[7]For an account of Wittgenstein's comparison of his later philosophy with relativity, see Stickney (2008a).

as he underwent training in engineering (Hamilton, 55), it also risks violating his admonitions to avoid 'our craving for generalization' (BB 18) and excessive theorizing (PI §108), where it is all too easy to conclude that 'it must be like this' (CV 37) and settle too hastily on causal explanations. Here, then, in the 'engineering-training hypothesis' is one of those captivating pictures Wittgenstein would free us from, as well as the tendency to posit an explanatory theory when an apt description would suffice. Talking about 'Wittgenstein's education' in relation to his philosophy we hope to avoid this kind of contradiction with his own expressed thinking.

Although opening an interesting and relevant line of inquiry, Fitzgerald (2004) also ventures too far, it seems, in trying to explain Wittgenstein's philosophical writing on language and psychology as the product of his High Functioning Autism and possibly Asperger's disease—conditions that likely account for his at times unusual behaviour, such as talking to himself, obsessive-compulsive attention to details, or flying off into fits of rage. These kinds of speculations are no doubt interesting and do round out a picture of the man whom we have come to know from his letters as deeply disturbed, lonely and often suicidal. As a psycho-biographical thesis, however, Fitzgerald then feels compelled to attack cultural explanations for Wittgenstein's appearance on the intellectual scene. It is more than a coincidence, however, that Wittgenstein saw himself in a kind of relationship to Freud (who analysed Wittgenstein's sister), referring to himself at one point as Freud's 'disciple', even although Wittgenstein increasingly divested himself of the tradition of scientific rationalism to which Freud belonged (see his "Conversations on Freud," LC 41–52; Cioffi 1998). With at least two, and possibly three of his older brothers committing suicide, the topic came very close to home for the often depressed and suicidal philosopher. He described himself to his sister Hermine as a man you see outside the closed window, not fully grasping what kind of storm is causing his strange movements and undermining him (Monk 1990, 170). Wittgenstein often wrote about psychology, 'mental states' and emotions: not only in his *Remarks on the Philosophy of Psychology* that make it into Part 2 of the *Investigations* but also in a variety of other texts (LPP, LW and LC) where he tried to develop a clear survey of problematic psychological concepts (Hacker 2010; Bellucci 2013; Rosenman and Nasti 2012). As a consequence of this preoccupation, bound up with his own life and his locale, there is a huge secondary literature dealing with these issues.

There are relatively few authors, however, who talk overtly about Wittgenstein's homosexuality (among the exceptions, see Peters 2017; Rejali 2017). Wittgenstein's uneasy sexuality, his relationships to David Pinsent, Ben Richards, Francis Skinner, his proposed marriage to Marguerite and even his non-sexual relationships with his disciples all point to the complexities inherent in approaching this topic: perhaps one reason why, for all its significance, philosophers have been noticeable by their reluctance to tackle it. Clearly, Wittgenstein's homosexuality is of central importance in understanding the man. The more difficult question is the effects of his homosexuality on his philosophy and on his relationships when he was a teacher.[8] Bartley uses the concept of façade to talk of its disguised effects of his inner states. Psychoanalytically, much could be made of this personal secrecy and the need to preserve confessional material from prying eyes that might be very damaging. Bartley (1983, 13) also refers to Steiner on *eros* and language—'sex is a profoundly semantic act'.

Monk (2001, 5) explicitly warns against the dangers of writing philosophical biography that tries to go beyond description to purport a theory of how a given philosopher such as Wittgenstein emerged. One can only write philosophical biography, he argues, for those who are capable of 'seeing connections'—not for those who are 'aspect-blind' or lack the expert judgment needed to weigh often 'imponderable evidence' (citing PI §122; PI, p. 227–28). As with art connoisseurs, only for those sufficiently immersed in the art form and its broader cultural background can one 'give intimations' and expect the other to understand them (Monk 2001, 6; citing LW 1, §927). Wittgenstein felt that this kind of understanding cannot be formally or explicitly taught: one can only provide tips as it were, and expertly model the correct procedure. Much of the evidence informing such refined judgment is 'imponderable' or ineffable (PI, p. 228). Wittgenstein grounds judgment of emotion and intention, for instance, in percipience and oversight (*übersicht*, or synopsis; cf. PI §122): 'Corrector prognoses will generally issue from the judgments of those with better knowledge of mankind' (PI, p. 227).

> To be sure, there is this: acquiring a knowledge of human nature; it is also possible to help someone with this, to give lessons, as it were, but one only points to cases, refers to certain traits, gives no hard and fast rules. (RPP, II §607; cf. PI, p. 227)

Accordingly, our task here is to widen the readership base for receiving these 'intimations' within various academic branches of educational research, not just philosophy of education, and so to make Wittgenstein's later thought more accessible—not as theory of education, but as a mode of critical thinking and a particular philosophical inclination or way of life (see Peters 2002). Before proceeding, however, we need more background on the early Wittgenstein and his inclination towards 'quietism', with which he wrestled continuously in his later philosophical work.

[8]See Albert W. Levi (1978–79) who sees Wittgenstein's ethics as a reflection of his guilty homosexuality.

## 1.3 Wittgenstein's *Tractatus* (1922) and the Vienna Circle (1926–29)

In the interim years between first studying at Cambridge (1912) and later returning to teach there in the Philosophy Department (1929), Wittgenstein first took refuge in a remote hut in Norway (1913) and then (after enlisting in the Austrian army) was interred in an Italian prison camp during World War I: during which time Wittgenstein wrote a short book (75 pages) that attempted to sum up everything that could be meaningfully said, passing over the rest in silence. The *Tractatus Logico-Philosophicus,* completed in 1918, expounded a theory of the general proposition: what can be expressed (or pictured) by language (and thought) and what can only be shown in the logic of syntax. It was published first in German in 1921 and later as a bilingual edition in 1922 with an introduction from Bertrand Russell, though Wittgenstein felt that neither Russell or Moore really understood what he was saying. In his *Tractatus*, Wittgenstein thought he had solved all the problems of modern philosophy by demonstrating the linguistic boundary between sense and nonsense.

> The aim of the book is to set a limit to thought, or rather — not to thought, but to the expression of thoughts: for in order to be able to set a limit to thought, we should have to find both sides of the limit thinkable (i.e. we should have to be able to think what cannot be thought).
>
> It will therefore only be in language that the limit can be set, and what lies on the other side of the limit will simply be nonsense. (TLP, Preface)
>
> Philosophy aims at the logical clarification of thoughts. Philosophy is not a body of doctrine but an activity. A philosophical work consists essentially of elucidations. Philosophy does not result in 'philosophical propositions', but rather in the clarification of propositions. Without philosophy thoughts are, as it were, cloudy and indistinct: its task is to make them clear and to give them sharp boundaries. (TLP 4.112)

Some of the topics about which he initially thought we cannot speak meaningfully were religion, ethics and aesthetics (TLP 6.421)[9]—topics he was especially fond of contemplating (see Harris 2017; Quinn 2017). In accord with this belief that he had delineated what could be meaningfully said, he gave up philosophy and enrolled in the teachers' training college in Vienna in 1919, taking up his first job as an elementary teacher in Trattenbach, a small rural mountain village in Austria. He shifted schools several times (Hassbach, Puchberg, Otterthal) only to resign abruptly from teaching after an incident (the so-called Haidbauer incident) that involve hitting an 11-year old boy for which he was called to trial in 1926 but resigned voluntarily instead. We return to this trying episode in his life in Chap. 3, and there explore how the concept of 'training' came to figure centrally in his later philosophy. After leaving teaching the reclusive Wittgenstein worked briefly as a gardener in a monastery.

---

[9]'Ethics and aesthetics are one and the same'. Ludwig Wittgenstein (TLP 6.421).

Following the publication of his *Tractatus*, Wittgenstein's reputation as a philosopher grew considerably. He briefly became a somewhat legendary figure within what is today referred to as the 'Vienna Circle' of logical positivism. How well Wittgenstein fit into this club is problematic; he respected and had a natural sympathy for the movement's founder Moritz Schlick (Oberdan 2013), a former student of Max Planck in Berlin and author of such monumental works as *Space and Time in Contemporary Physics* (1917), and *General Theory of Knowledge* (1922). Schlick counselled the members on how *not* to irritate Wittgenstein upon his early reception into the group, having come to understand his delicacy while negotiating with his sister Margarete Stonborough Wittgenstein for a visit (Oberdan 2013). Wittgenstein shared an interest in mathematics with notable members like Kurt Gödel, whose view of mathematics as being like a game governed by its axioms fits well with Wittgenstein's later views (in LFM, c. 1938–9) on the arbitrariness of rules—a position that frustrated Alan Turing. Many notable figures were also affiliated with this school, such as the physicist Hans Reichenbach in Germany. A. J. Ayer at Oxford (1936) identified strongly with the *Tractatus* and felt that Wittgenstein was supporting him when he presented papers for the Moral Sciences Club at Cambridge (Ayer 2016, 683). In his influential book, *Language, Truth and Logic* (1936), Ayer also expressed an affinity with some of the more extreme logical positivists, citing Rudolf Carnap who like the empiricist David Hume would burn any books dealing with subjects beyond the reach of verification through science, such as religion; in Carnap's and Ayer's case, Heidegger's metaphysical writings in *Being and Time* should go onto the pyre. Wittgenstein avoided contact with Carnap, and in a letter to Schlick's student Friedrich Waismann (who travelled with them and kept notes of their meetings), Wittgenstein expressed his antipathy to Carnap's caustic view.

> I can very well think what Heidegger meant about *Being* and *Angst*. Man has the drive to run up against the boundaries of language….
>
> But the tendency to run up against shows something. The holy Augustine already knew this when he said: "What, you scoundrel, you would speak no nonsense? Go ahead and speak nonsense – it doesn't matter!" (LWVC 68)

In a letter to Drury (in Rhees 1981) he once remarked that he was not really opposed to metaphysics, though he confessed not to have read Aristotle which seemed odd even to him, as a Cambridge philosopher. Instead of this philosophical genre, he was more concerned with everyday abusage of language and had Drury collect for him articles that seemed to typify what he called 'language on holiday' (PI §38).

When Wittgenstein attended the Circle, he sometimes read loudly the poetry of Tagore, pointing to higher realizations that language (on his own account) was supposed to be incapable of capturing. Wittgenstein once tried to clarify the apparent contradiction in a letter to Paul Engelmann (1967): 'The poem by Uhland is really magnificent. And that is how it is: if only you do not try to utter what is unutterable then *nothing* gets lost. (But the unutterable will be—unutterably—contained in what has been uttered.)' Cryptically, Wittgenstein embraced Longfellow's sentiment that 'the gods are everywhere', altering the poet's phrase in making this 'his motto' (CV 34e; see Smith 2017, and Longfellow, 'The Golden Milestone'). Engelmann elaborates on the disjunction:

> Positivism holds – and this is its essence – that what we can speak about is all that matters in life. Whereas Wittgenstein passionately believes that all that really matters in human life is precisely what, in his views, we must be silent about. When he nevertheless takes immense pains to delimit the unimportant, it is not the coastline of that island which he is bent on surveying with such meticulous accuracy, but the boundary of the ocean. (Engelmann 1967, 97)

In this appreciation of the vast 'ocean' beyond, Wittgenstein differed in sentiment from the more empirically minded positivists.

In 1929 Wittgenstein was persuaded by Ramsay and Keynes to return to Cambridge following the horrendous events that accompanied his abrupt resignation from his teaching post (Peters 2017; see Ch 3). Russell suggested that he offer the *Tractatus* as a Ph.D. dissertation. He was examined by Russell and Moore, whom Wittgenstein remarked did not understand the work and never would, and he became a lecturer and fellow of Trinity. In 1929, Wittgenstein gave 'A Lecture on Ethics' at Cambridge for the Heretics Society (of which his lover David Pinsent was a member). He later discussed the lecture with the Vienna Circle (see editor's note, PO 36).

What Wittgenstein said in his 'Lecture on Ethics' (LE, in PO)—the only other work published in his lifetime—is that anything we might consider miraculous, such as somebody sprouting a lion's head (his example), would soon become just another fact of natural science in our world: it would be describable in our language, as are other facts or pieces of information. This idea appears also in his *Remarks on Frazer's Golden Bough* (PO, RFM 129), where he remarked that 'no phenomenon is in itself particularly mysterious, but any of them can become so to us, and the characteristic feature of the awakening mind of man is precisely the fact that a phenomenon comes to have meaning for him.' Drury recalls how Wittgenstein disliked James Jeans' title for his popular book on cosmology, *The Mysterious Universe*, as there is really nothing mysterious about astronomy and theoretical physics (see LC 27, and Stickney 2008 on Wittgenstein's references to Einstein's relativity theory). Furthermore, although in some cases we use words like 'good' as similes: 'he's a good man' being fashioned after 'that's a good chair', in ethical and religious language we don't really have a word that would replace the simile (as we do when an advertisement says 'a good truck is like a horse', i.e. that it's a strong, fast and dependable friend worth having). The kind of irreducible similes he had in mind are absolute ones (the good or the beautiful), and such mystical or ineffable experiences as sensing (grasping) the existence of the world and feeling completely safe.

> Our words used as we use them in science, are vessels capable only of containing and conveying meaning and sense, natural meaning and sense. Ethics, if it is anything, is supernatural and our words will only express facts; as a teacup will only hold a teacup full of water and if I were to pour out a gallon over it. I said that so far as facts and propositions are concerned there is only relative value and relative good, right, etc. (PO: LE 40)

Wittgenstein goes further, showing what he considered to be the boundary between sense and nonsense in language.

> The truth is that the scientific way of looking at a fact is not the way to look at it as a miracle. For imagine whatever fact you may, it is not in itself miraculous in the absolute sense of that term. For we see now that we have been using the word 'miracle' in a relative and an absolute sense. And I will now describe the experience of wondering at the existence of the world by saying: it is the experience of seeing the world as a miracle. Now I am tempted to say that the right expression in language for the miracle of the existence of the world, though it is not any proposition *in* language, is the existence of language itself. But then what does it mean to be aware of this miracle at some times and not at other times? For all I have said by shifting the expression of the miraculous from an expression *by means of* language to the expression *by the existence* of language, all I have said is again that we cannot express what we want to express and that all we *say* about the absolute miraculous remains nonsense. (PO: LE 43–44)

The word 'nonsense' here does not have the ordinary sense of being ridiculous, but of being logically outside the world of language (like his propositions about the world or space of language).[10] It was not meant to have a pejorative sense, as he made clear in concluding remarks (see Burbules and Smeyers 2003).

> That is to say: I see now that these nonsensical expressions were not nonsensical because I had not yet found the correct expressions, but that their nonsensicality was their very essence. For all I wanted to do with them was just *to go beyond* the world and that is to say beyond significant language. My whole tendency and I believe the tendency of all men who ever tried to write or talk Ethics or Religion was to run against the boundaries of language. This running against the walls of our cage is perfectly, absolutely hopeless. Ethics so far as it springs from the desire to say something about the ultimate meaning of life, the absolute good, the absolute valuable, can be no science. What it says does not add to our knowledge in any sense. But it is a document of a tendency in the human mind which I personally cannot help respecting deeply and I would not for my life ridicule it. (PO LE, p. 44)

That he did not intend a kind of scientific reductionism (of the ocean to the island of the sayable) is clear from remarks like these (c. 1930), which Gordon Bearm (1997, 160–67) reads instead as an extension of Nietzsche's early existentialism:

> Man has to awaken to wonder—and so perhaps do peoples. Science is a way of sending him to sleep again. (CV 5e)

Although trained as an engineer and highly respectful of the sciences, the problems of science no longer captured his imagination; nor could they address the kinds of problems he wanted to entertain, such as matters of perception (seeing emotions on the faces of others). As we noted earlier, he was fond of inquiries into religion (see LC), and into ethics and aesthetics (which he equated in the *Tractatus*,

[10]Max Black (1964, 380–81) explains that this was also true for the early Wittgenstein of the *Tractatus*. 'The word "senseless", practically a synonym for "nonsensical" in ordinary English, strongly suggests something improper, absurd, and useless.... In his intended meaning, "senseless" is not always used pejoratively, as is clearly shown by his contention that logical and mathematical statements are all "senseless" (4.461)...'

TLP 6.421): the kinds of topics he earlier said in his 'Lecture on Ethics' we could not speak of meaningfully (PO 44).

> Nothing could be more remarkable than seeing a man who thinks he is unobserved performing some quite simple everyday activity. . . . [This is] something more wonderful than anything a playwright could arrange to be acted or spoken on the stage: life itself. —But then we do see this every day without its making the slightest impression on us! True enough, but we do not see it from that point of view. . . . Only an artist can represent an individual thing as to make it appear to us like a work of art. . . . A work of art forces us—as one might say—to see it in the right perspective but, in the absence of art, the object is just a fragment of nature like any other. . . (CV 4–5e)
>
> You really could call it, not exactly the expression of a feeling, but a least an expression of feeling, or a felt expression. And you could say too that insofar as people understand it, they 'resonate' in harmony with it, responds to it. You might say: the work of art does not aim to convey *something else*, just itself. (CV 58e)

Throughout his life, Wittgenstein repeatedly found himself caught in this conflict between trying to reside within the limits of human understanding, adhering to sensibility and the 'respectable tendency' to mystically reach beyond (LE, in PO 43–44). His original preface to his *Remarks on Fraser's Golden Bough*, which he later removed as it registered with him as 'crap', he reflects on his earlier project in the *Tractatus*:

> *I now believe that it would be right to begin my book with remarks about metaphysics as a kind of magic.*
>
> *But in doing this I must not make a case for magic nor may I make fun of it.*
>
> *The depth of magic should be preserved.* —
>
> *Indeed, here the elimination of magic has itself the character of magic.*
>
> For, back then, when I began talking about the 'world' (and not about this tree or table), what else did I want but to keep something higher spellbound in my words? (RFGB, in PO 116–17)

To better understand what he is saying here, consider these concluding phrases in the *Tractatus*:

> The solution of the riddle of life in space and time lies outside space and time. (It is certainly not the solution of any problems of natural science that is required.) (TLP 6.4312)
>
> There, are, indeed, things that cannot be put into words. They are what is mystical. (TLP 6.522)
>
> The correct method in philosophy would really be the following: to say nothing except what can be said, i.e. propositions of natural science – i.e., something that has nothing to do with philosophy – and then, whenever someone else wanted to say something metaphysical, to demonstrate to him that he had failed to give meaning to certain signs in his propositions. Although it would not be satisfactory to the other person – he would not have the feeling that we were teaching him philosophy – *this* method would be the only strictly correct one. (TLP 6.53)
>
> My propositions serve as elucidations in the following way: anyone who understands me eventually recognizes them as nonsensical, when he has used them – as steps – to climb up beyond them. He must, so to speak, throw away the ladder after he has climbed up it. (TLP 6.54; see Maruyama 2017, on elucidations)

What we cannot speak about we must pass over in silence. (TLP 7)

Again, in a letter to Englemann, Wittgenstein clarifies how we are to receive these mystical utterances in the *Tractatus*, whether this was in fact his original intent or a bit of revisionist history on his part (an author actively fashioning the reception of his troubling verse).

> The book's point is an ethical one. I once meant to include in the preface a sentence which is not in fact there now but which I will write out for you here, because it will perhaps be a key to work for you. What I meant to write, then, was this: My work consists of two parts: the one presented here plus all that I have not written. And it is precisely this second part that is the important one. My book draws the limits to the sphere of the ethical from the inside as it were, and I am convinced that this is the only rigorous way of drawing those limits. In short, I believe that where many others today are just gassing, I have managed in my book to put everything firmly into place by being silent about it. (Englemann 1967, 143–44)

## 1.4 Wittgenstein as a Philosophy Teacher: His Return to Cambridge (1929–1947)[11]

> A present-day teacher of philosophy doesn't select food for his pupil with the aim of flattering his taste, but with the aim of changing it. (CV 17e)

> One repays one's teacher badly if one always remains nothing but a pupil. (Nietzsche 1966: 78)

Cambridge offered a sanctuary from the gossip that surrounded Wittgenstein as an elementary teacher in small Austrian mountain villages. It was a place of refuge, a known place where he was supported by friends. It was also the place where in conversation with Russell and Moore, Wittgenstein had become famous for the birth of 'analytic philosophy'. Yet almost immediately Wittgenstein began working through his own doubts about his early work, departing from the realm of pure logic to pursue questions of actual language use and meaning within practices or 'language-games'. This was an extraordinary departure that turned its back on the movement of logicism and on the picture-theory of meaning to embrace a form of philosophical anthropology emphasizing 'meaning-as-use' within communities.

Wittgenstein lectured without notes but some of the content of his lectures comes down to us through accounts offered by his students. From these recollections, there seems to be a continuity between his style of teaching and his philosophical writing. Consequently, his lectures and student notes have become part of his posthumous corpus of writings. At another level of composition his 'notes' are sometimes reworked in the process of dictation, comprising preliminary notebooks for his later writing project, the *Investigations*:

---

[11]This section draws on material from Peters (2001).

> The accounts of his teaching by his students confirm an *intensity* of thinking that shows itself in his writings; this intensity is driven, in large part, by the ethical and aesthetic requirements of *arranging* or composing his thoughts. His writings mirror his approach to teaching philosophy and vice versa. Above all they reflect his *honesty* as a thinker and teacher. And if he was unforgiving in his treatment of his students, it is because he was unforgiving with himself. The long painful silences that interspersed his classes, his disregard for institutional conventions in pedagogy at the time and his relentless (self) criticism were an essential part of his style as a "great educator" (in Nietzsche's sense). (Peters 2001)

Accounts of Wittgenstein as a teacher of philosophy are now legendary. D. A. T. Gasking and A. C. Jackson (1967, 51) report the following description Wittgenstein gave of his own teaching:

> In teaching you philosophy I'm like a guide showing you how to find your way round London. I have to take you through the city from north to south, from east to west, from Euston to the embankment and from Piccadilly to the Marble Arch. After I have taken you many journeys through the city, in all sorts of directions, we shall have passed through any given street a number of times – each time traversing the street as part of a different journey. At the end of this you will know London; you will be able to find your way about like a Londoner. Of course, a good guide will take you through the more important streets more often than he takes you down side streets; a bad guide will do the opposite. In philosophy I'm a rather bad guide …. (see Ch 2.1, re: Geography)

Gasking and Jackson (1967, 50) focus on the 'technique of oral discussion' that Wittgenstein utilizes, a technique they describe as, at first, bewildering:

> Example was piled up on example. Sometimes the examples were fantastic, as when one was invited to consider the very odd linguistic or other behaviour of an imaginary tribe … Sometimes the example was just a reminder of some well-known homely fact. Always the case was given in concrete detail, described in down-to-earth everyday language. Nearly every single thing said was easy to follow and was usually not the sort of thing anyone would wish to dispute.

The difficulty came from seeing where this 'repetitive concrete' talk was leading. Although lecturing without notes, each session was nevertheless carefully planned. Sometimes he 'would break off, saying "Just a minute, let me think!" … or he would exclaim "This is as difficult as *hell*"' (Gasking and Jackson 1967, 52). Sometimes the point of the many examples became suddenly clear as though the solution was obvious and simple. They report Wittgenstein as saying that he wanted to show his students that they had confusions that they never thought they could have and admonished them by saying: 'You must say what you really think as though no one, not even you, could overhear it' (53). And Gasking and Jackson make the enormously important remark: 'Whether this ideal is realisable in the form of a book is, in the opinion of many, not yet known; whether, if it were, the book would look much like what we think of as a philosophy book is discussible' (53). Wittgenstein was clearly experimenting with the form his remarks should take: he is to be distinguished as a great philosopher not only for his thinking, or for his *styles* of philosophizing, but for his deliberate attention to and constant (perhaps, obsessive) experimentation with philosophical form and genre.

G. E. Moore (1967, 44) in his memory of Wittgenstein's lectures during the period 1930–33, writes:

> I was a good deal surprised by some of the things he [Wittgenstein] said about the difference between 'philosophy' in the sense in which what he was doing might be called 'philosophy' (he called this 'modern philosophy'), and what has traditionally been called 'philosophy'. He said what he was doing was a 'new subject' which Wittgenstein said did resemble traditional philosophy in three respects: in its generality, in the fact that it was fundamental to both ordinary life and the sciences, and in that it was independent of the results of science.

Moore confirms the picture of Wittgenstein as an innovator when it came to 'doing philosophy'. Wittgenstein is to be construed as 'doing philosophy' equally when he is teaching as when he is writing and Wittgenstein went to great pains to develop a style in the form of his philosophical investigations that enables the reader to think for him- or herself.

Karl Britton (1967, 61) reports that Wittgenstein thought there was no test one could apply to discover whether a philosopher was teaching properly: 'He said that many of his pupils merely put forward his own ideas: and that many of them imitated his voice and manner; but that he could easily distinguish those who really understood.' Wittgenstein urged his students not to become philosophers or to take up academic posts first because he had scant regard for professional philosophers and because philosophical thinking is strenuous with 'long periods of darkness and confusion' (Fann 1967, 69).

There are many other recollections of Wittgenstein as a philosophy teacher which testify to the way his style of thinking and teaching had dramatically changed in the last 20 years of his life and how his teaching was mirrored or *embodied* in his work (see, in particular, the contributions of Malcolm and Rhees in Fann's 1967 collection). They call into question our traditional notion of a 'work' in the same way that Michel Foucault and Roland Barthes question the notion of an 'author'. Doing philosophy always took priority for Wittgenstein whether this was in oral or written form: it was important to show the deep puzzles in our language (culture and thinking) as well as dissolving them by 'doing'. Doing philosophy 'let the fly out of the fly-bottle' (PI §310): it cured our buzzing confusion and allowed us to lead useful and practical lives.

Norman Malcolm offers candid remarks on Wittgenstein the professor, in reviewing Rhees' book 'Recollections'.

> Was Wittgenstein a good university teacher? Leavis did not think so. He never attended Wittgenstein's lectures: but he knew some of the young men who did, and saw no evidence that Wittgenstein's influence resulted in 'fortified intellectual powers'. Leavis didn't believe that any of the students, or even mature philosophers, who attended were able to be serious collaborators in the discussions. He thought that 'the wonder and the profit for the lecture-audience lay in the opportunity to witness the sustained spontaneous effort of intellectual genius wrestling with its self-proposed problems.' Perhaps this was true in many cases. But there was another kind of influence. John King, an under-graduate member of those classes and a friend, viewed Wittgenstein 'as a man of high moral, intellectual and artistic integrity … tolerant of those who had less ability than himself and never censorious except of what he considered humbug, hypocrisy, affectation'. King believed that

> Wittgenstein 'saw a high seriousness and purpose in life', and he quotes his words: 'Of one thing I am certain – we are not here in order to have a good time.' (Malcolm 1981)

Von Wright's depiction concurs with Malcolm's, also noting his interrogative style of teaching

> From the beginning of 1930 Wittgenstein lectured at Cambridge. As might be expected, his lectures were highly 'unacademic'. He nearly always held them in his own room, or in the college rooms of a friend. He had no manuscript or note. He *thought* before the class. The impression was of tremendous concentration. (Von Wright, 1982, 29)

At first jesting that, 'It need not surprise us that Wittgenstein's restless genius was not happy in academic routines' (30), Von Wright then noted that Wittgenstein was disturbed by the sectarian allegiances of his pupils: 'This caused Wittgenstein much pain. He thought that his influence as a teacher was, on the whole, harmful to the development of independent minds in his discipline. I'm afraid he was right' (1982, 31). Although praising his 'pure seriousness and powerful intelligence' (32), he presents the image of an impressive but not entirely successful educator (a view supported by Burwood 2017).

> Because of the depth and originality of his thinking, it is very difficult to understand Wittgenstein's ideas and even more difficult to incorporate them into one's thinking. At the same time the magic of his personality and style was most inviting and persuasive. To learn from Wittgenstein without coming to adapt his forms of expression and catchwords and even to imitate his tone of voice, his mien and gestures, was almost impossible. The danger was that the thoughts should deteriorate into jargon. The teaching of great men often has a simplicity and naturalness which makes the difficult appear easy to grasp. Their disciples usually become therefore, insignificant epigones. The historical significance of such men does not manifest itself in their disciples but through influences of a more indirect, subtle, and often unexpected kind. (Von Wright 1982, 31–2)

Regardless of his efficacy as a professor, during this period while Wittgenstein lectured at Cambridge (1929–1947), he developed the collections of remarks and preparatory notebooks that we receive today as texts conveying his later philosophy: including a late edition of fragmentary remarks entitled *Zettel*, which means literally 'scraps'. Escaping again to the remote hut in Norway (see Rejali 2017), Wittgenstein meticulously crafted the typescripts that were later published posthumously in 1953 as the *Philosophical Investigations,* in which he set out to demolish his own work in the earlier *Tractatus*.

> Where does our investigation get its importance from, since it seems only to destroy everything, that is, all that is great and important? (As it were, all the buildings, leaving behind only bits of stone and rubble.) What we are destroying is nothing but houses of cards and we are clearing up the ground of language on which they stand. (PI §118)

> Each of the sentences I write is trying to say the whole thing, i.e., the same thing over and over again; it is as though they were all simply views of one object seen from different angles.

> I might say: if the place I want to get to could only be reached by way of a ladder, I would give up trying to get there. For the place I really have to get to is a place I must already be at now.

> Anything that I might reach by climbing a ladder does not interest me. ('Sketch for a Foreword' to his *Philosophical Remarks*, in CV 6–7e)

> (All that philosophy can do is to destroy idols. And that means not creating a new one – for instance as in "absence of an idol".) (PO, Phil., 171)

Strangely, he again concluded that his remarks in the *Philosophical Investigations* were useful in so far as they help us to stop doing philosophy when we want to (PI §132), and that his shift in attention to philosophical grammar again meant an end to philosophy.

> If one tried to advance *theses* in philosophy, it would never be possible to debate them, because everyone would agree to them. (PI §128)

In spite of seeking a terminus for philosophy instead of advancing bold claims on the meaning of life, both the *Tractatus* and the *Investigations* have been hailed as masterpieces. There are important continuities and differences between these early and later works, as well as in the volume of later remarks collected in *On Certainty*. After his death in 1951, Wittgenstein's *Nachlass* (WT) have been progressively released including the electronic edition of his complete works (Wittgenstein 2000)—some 20,000 pages of unpublished manuscripts. Not surprisingly, a whole industry was built around the interpretation of this corpus, which also includes his collected lectures notes (often taken by students) and his letters.

That Wittgenstein retained and yet modified earlier views on the boundaries of sensible language shows in his preservation of the underlying motif, here in his later collection entitled *Philosophy* (c. 1933, in PO):

> Again and again there is the attempt to define the world in language and to display it – but that doesn't work. The self-evidence of the world is expressed in the very fact that language means only it, and can mean only it.

> As language gets its way of meaning from what it means, from the world, no language is thinkable which doesn't represent this world. (PO, Phil., p. 193)

> The results of philosophy are the uncovering of one or another piece of plain nonsense, and are the bumps that the understanding has got by running its head against the limits // the end // of language. These bumps let us *understand* // recognize // the value of the discovery. (PO, Phil., 187)

> The real foundations of his inquiry do not strike a man at all. Unless that fact has at some time struck him // he has become aware of//. (Frazer, etc., etc.)

> And this means he fails to be struck by what is most striking (powerful). (PO, Phil., 179)

> (One of the greatest impediments for philosophy is the expectation of new, deep // unheard of // elucidations.) (PO, Phil., 179)

In the *Philosophical Investigations*, generally taken to be the most authoritative source for Wittgenstein's later thought as he worked to compile the manuscripts, we find similar themes.

> The results of philosophy are the uncovering of one or another piece of plain nonsense and of the bumps that the understanding has got by running its head against the limits of language. (PI §119)

> It is true to say that our considerations could not be scientific ones. …And we may not advance any kind of theory. There must not be anything hypothetical in our considerations. We must do away with all *explanation*, and description alone must take its place. And this description gets its light, that is to say its purpose, from philosophical problems. These are not, of course, empirical problems: they are solved, rather, by looking into the workings of our language, and that in such a way as to make us recognise those workings: in spite of an urge to misunderstand them. The problems are solved, not by giving new information, but by arranging what we have always known. Philosophy is a battle against the bewitchment of our intelligence by means of language. (PI §109)
>
> Philosophy simply puts everything before us and neither explains nor deduces anything. Since everything lies open there is nothing to explain. For what is hidden, for example, is of no use to us. (PI §126)

## 1.5 Conclusion: 'Scenes of Instruction' in the Later Wittgenstein

How, then, did the rather enigmatic Wittgenstein come to occupy the attention of some philosophers of education after his death in 1951, and why is he still important today? A brief excursus will serve to illustrate why his later philosophy has relevancy for education. Though some commentators might deny this relevancy, we were pleased that David Bakhurst (2017) decided in the affirmative in is Foreword to our recent book. Where to start, but with his opening reflections on Augustine's description of how children come to learn words, deficient from the get-go as he does not distinguish between different kinds of words or their contexts of usage (PI §1)?

> It is so difficult to find the beginning. Or, better: it is difficult to begin at the beginning. And not try to go further back. (OC §471)

The *Investigations* opens with a thought-experiment that reveals why Wittgenstein has gripped some philosophers of education: a scene in which we imagine builders working with a very simplistic language consisting of three words, the philosophical goal being to show how the representational view of language (see PI §1, re: Augustine) has become entrenched in our worldview or picture of language, and hence how a:

> general notion of the meaning of a word surrounds the working of language with a haze which makes clear vision impossible. It dispenses the fog to study the phenomena of language in primitive kinds of application in which one can command a clear view of the aim and functioning of words.
>
> A child uses such primitive forms of language when it learns to talk. Here the teaching of language is not explanation, but training. (PI §5)
>
> An important part of the training will consist in the teacher's pointing to the objects, directing the child's attention to them, and at the same time uttering a word; for instance, the word 'slab' as he points to that shape. (I do not want to call this "ostensive definition", because the child cannot as yet *ask* wat the name is. I will call it "ostensive teaching of words". – I say that it will form an important part of the training, because it is so with

> human beings; not because it could not be imagined otherwise.) This ostensive teaching of words can be said to establish an association between the word and thing. But what does this mean?… (PI §6)

He gradually shows us why this kind of *ostensive teaching* cannot on its own be effective in conveying the concept and works at best with nouns that describe things or people (PI §1).

> —Doubtless the ostensive teaching helped us to bring this about; but only with a particular training. With different training the same ostensive teaching of these words would have effected a quite different understanding.
>
> "I set the brake up by connecting up rod and lever." – Yes, given the whole of the rest of the mechanism. Only in conjunction with that is it a brake-lever, and separated from its support it is not even a lever; it may be anything, or nothing. (PI §6)[12]

Trained as an engineer, he characteristically selects a mechanical illustration to show how particular parts only have meaning when we have already acquired a sense as to the whole mechanism and its functioning. He later summarizes the lesson on semantic holism as follows:

> So one might say: the ostensive definition explains the use – the meaning – of the word when the overall role of the word in language is clear. (PI §30)

In order to arrive at this conclusion, he proceeds to show how learning the proper use of words like 'there' and 'this' cannot work as in ostensive teaching of the first five numerals, where one can set up a few objects and try to connect number sense with objects (e.g. 'here are three apples' takes for granted the meaning of the word 'here'). He then offers an analogy he retains throughout earlier (1930s) and later (1940s) writing.

> Think of the tools in a tool-box; there is a hammer, pliers, a saw, a screw-driver, a rule, a glue-pot, glue, nails and screws. – The functions of words are as diverse as the functions of these objects. (And in both cases there are similarities.)
>
> Of course, what confuses use is the uniform appearance of words when we hear them spoken or meet them in script and print. For their application is not presented to us so clearly. Especially when we are doing philosophy! (PI §11)

Developing his argument slowly by considering many examples or applications, he arrives at a crucial realization, also significant in that it introduces two of his central concepts: *language-games* and *forms of life*, the latter appearing only five times in the *Investigations* (PI §§19, 23, 241, and p. 174, p. 226; see Hacker 2015) and yet emblematic of his later thinking (OC §559) about how we are initiated into customary ways of being as we are acculturated into language.

> There are *countless* kinds: countless different kinds of use of what we call "symbols," "words," "sentences." And this multiplicity is not something fixed, given once for all; but

[12]Scenes of training to react normally also open his *Remarks on the Foundations of Mathematics,* where he questions how "people are brought by their education (training) so to use" formulas, and so "trained that all take the same step and the same point." (RFM I. 1–2)

> new types of language, new language-games, as we may say, come into existence, and others become obsolete and get forgotten. . . . Here the term "*language-game*" is meant to bring into prominence the fact that the *speaking* of language is part of an activity, or of a form of life.
>
> Review the multiplicity of language-game in the following examples, and in others:
>
> - Giving orders, and obeying them—
> - Describing the appearance of an object, or giving its measurements—
> - Constructing an object from a description (a drawing)—
> - Reporting an event—
> - Speculating about an event—
> - Forming and testing a hypothesis—
> - Presenting the results of an experiment in tables and diagrams—
> - Making up a story; and reading it—
> - Play-acting—
> - Singing catches—
> - Guessing riddles—
> - Making a joke; telling it—
> - Solving a problem in practical arithmetic—
> - Translating from one language into another—
> - Asking, thanking, cursing, greeting, praying.
>
> —It is interesting to compare the multiplicity of the tools in language and of the ways they are used, the multiplicity of kinds of word and sentence, with what logicians have said about the structure of language. (Including the author of the *Tractatus Logico-Philosophicus*.) (PI §23)

Wittgenstein's emphasis on the myriad uses of words and the multiplicity of *language-games* takes us from the realization of how meaning depends upon a vast background of now fossilized[13] and also living cultural context (*bedrock*) we have obtained through training (see Ch 2), to the equally significant understanding that meaning is governed by ways of language usage that have gradually become customary for us but which also change over time (see Ch 4)—allowing for new uses or contexts of usage to emerge and evolve.

> For a large class of cases—though not for all—in which we employ the word "meaning" it can be defined thus: the meaning of a word is its use in the language. (PI §43)
>
> Let the use of words teach you their meaning. (PI, p. 220)
>
> Isn't the question "Have these words a meaning?" similar to "Is that a tool?" asked as one produces, say, a hammer? I say "Yes, it's a hammer." But what if the thing that any of us would take for a hammer were somewhere else a missile, for example, or a conductor's baton? Now make the application yourself. (OC §351)

[13]The propositions of mathematics might be said to be fossilized.—The proposition 'I am called…' is not. But it too is regarded as *incontrovertible* by those who, like myself, have overwhelming evidence for it. And this is not out of thoughtlessness. For, the evidence's being overwhelming consists precisely in the fact that we do not *need* to give way before any contrary evidence. And so we have here a buttress similar to the one that makes the propositions of mathematics incontrovertible.

The question 'But mightn't you be in the grip of a delusion now and later find this out?'—might also be raised as an objection to any proposition of the multiplication table. (OC §512)

> …A meaning of a word is a kind of employment of it. For it is what we learn when the word is incorporated into our language. (OC §61)
>
> If we imagine the facts otherwise than as they are, certain language-games lose some of their importance, while others become important. And in this way, there is an alteration – a gradual one – in the use of the vocabulary of a language. (OC §63)
>
> When language-games change, then there is a change in concepts, and with the concepts the meanings of words change. (OC §65)

There are two important points here: first, in the flow of thought or action we do not have recourse to explicit rules, but carry out meaningful speech and action through embodied or tacit reason we have acquired through training. Wittgenstein repeatedly makes this point by stating that at some point in any search for a rational explanation, 'reasons give out', and we simply act in such-and-such ways without reasons (PI §§211, 217, 654). Second, there is no single definition of terms such as 'good' or 'teaching' to which we can refer (after the fact, or analytically) in describing what, say, 'good teaching' is, but a family or range of familiar usages (see PI §68). By focusing on actual practices instead of ideals, Wittgenstein sets himself in opposition to essentialist philosophy—as the antithesis of Socrates[14]:

> I cannot characterise my standpoint better than by saying that it is opposed to that which Socrates represents in the Platonic dialogues. For if asked what knowledge is I would list examples of knowledge, and add the words 'and the like'. No common element is to be found in all of them (Unpublished Manuscript 302; in Hallet 1977)[15]

Instead of looking for underlying criteria for meaning, Wittgenstein asks us to consider the teaching of these words.

> How did we *learn* the meaning of this word ("good" for instance)? From what sort of examples? in what language games? Then it will be easier for you to see that the word must have a family of meanings. (PI §77)

## References

Ayer, A. J. (1936). *Language, truth and logic*. London: Victor Gollancz Ltd.

Ayer, A. J. (2016). Recollections of Wittgenstein. In F. A. Flowers & Ian Ground (Eds.), *Portraits of Wittgenstein* (Vol. 2, pp. 682–686). London, Oxford, New York: Bloomsbury Academic.

Bakhurst, D. (2017). Wittgenstein and education (Foreword). In M. A. Peters & J. Stickney (Eds.), *A companion to Wittgenstein on education: Pedagogical investigations*, v–xiii. Singapore: Springer.

Bartley, W., III. (1973). *Wittgenstein*. London: Quartet Books.

---

[14]It has puzzled me why Socrates is regarded as a great philosopher. Because when Socrates asks for the meaning of a word and people give him examples of how that word is used, he isn't satisfied but wants a unique definition. Now if someone shows me how a word is used and its different meanings, that is just the sort of answer I want. (PG VI, 76)

[15]BT—Wittgenstein, "Big Typescript" MS 213, 423, in G.H. von Wright, "*The Wittgenstein Papers*", 483–503.

Bartley, W., III. (1983/1992). Wittgenstein and homosexuality. Revised version of the "Afterword 1982" to German and Spanish translations of *Wittgenstein*, Salmagundi, No. 58/59 (Fall 1982–Winter 1983), pp. 166–196.
Bearn, G. (1997). *Waking to wonder: Wittgenstein's existential investigations*. Albany, New York: Stature University of New York Press.
Bellucci, F. (2013). Wittgenstein's grammar of emotions. *RIFL, 13*(1): 1–7. At www.rifl.unical.it/index.php/rifl/article/view/2/2.
Biletzki, A. (2002). Ludwig Wittgenstein. *Stanford Encyclopedia of Philosophy*. https://plato.stanford.edu/entries/wittgenstein/.
Black, M. (1964). A companion to Wittgenstein's. *Tractatus'*. Ithica, N.Y.: Cornell Unhiversity Press.
Britton, K. (1967). Portrait of a philosopher. In K. T. Fann (Ed.), *Ludwig Wittgenstein: The man and his philosophy*. New York: Dell (also, New Jersey: Humanities Press; and, Sussex: Harvester Press.)
Burbules, N., & Smeyers, P. (2003). The later Wittgenstein and ethics: Invigorating questions challenging the outlook on education. *Philosophy of Education, 58,* 248–257.
Burbules, N. C., & Peters, M. A. (2003). Tractarian pedagogies: Sense and nonsense. Translated and published as "Pedagogias tractarianas: Sentido y sinsentido," *Revista Discusiones Filosoficas (Spain), 4*(7), 51–65.
Burwood, S. (2017). "A spontaneous following": Wittgenstein, education and the limits of trust. In M. A. Peters & J. Stickney (Eds.), *A companion to Wittgenstein on education: Pedagogical investigations*, 161–177. Singapore: Springer.
Cavell. J. (1979). *The claim of reason*. Wittgenstein, skepticism, morality and tragedy. New York: Oxford University Press.
Child, W. (2011). *Wittgenstein*. New York and Abington, UK: Routledge.
Cioffi, F. (1998). Information, contemplation and social life. In *Wittgenstein on Freud and Frazer* (Chap. 1, 19–46). Cambridge: Cambridge University Press.
Drury, M. O. (1967). A symposium: Assessments of the man and the philosopher. In K. T. Fann (ed.), *Ludwig Wittgenstein: The man and his philosophy*. New York: Dell.
Drury, M. O. (1981). Some notes on conversations with Wittgenstein. In R. Rhees (Ed.), *Ludwig Wittgenstein: Personal recollections*. Oxford: Blackwell.
Engelmann, P. (1967). *Letters from Ludwig Wittgenstein* (L. Furtmuller, Trans.). Oxford: Basil Blackwell.
Fann, K. T. (1969). *Wittgenstein's conception of philosophy*. Oxford: Basil Blackwell.
Fitzgerald, M. (2000). Did Ludwig Wittgenstein have Asperger's syndrome? *European Child and Adolescent Psychiatry, 9*(1):61–65.
Fitzgerald, M. (2004). *Autism and creativity. Is there a link between autism in men and exceptional ability?* Hove and New York: Bruner-Routledge.
Gasking, D. A. T., & Jackson, A. C. (1967). Wittgenstein as a teacher. In K. T. Fann (Ed.), *Ludwig Wittgenstein: The man and his philosophy*, 49–55. Atlantic Highlands, NJ: Humanities Press.
Glock, H.-J. (1996). *A Wittgenstein dictionary*. Oxford: Blackwell.
Green, T. (1968). Topology of the teaching concept. In C. J. B. MacMillan & T. W. Nelson (Eds.), *Concepts of teaching*. Rand McNally: NewYork.
Harris, S. (2017). Imagination and reality in Wittgenstein's later philosophy. In M. A. Peters & J. Stickney (Eds.), *A companion to Wittgenstein on education: Pedagogical investigations* (pp. 135–146). Singapore: Springer.
Hacker, P. M. S. (2010). The development of Wittgenstein's philosophy of psychology. At http://info.sjc.ox.ac.uk/scr/hacker/docs/TheDevelopmentOfWittgensteinsPhilosophyOfPsychology.pdf.
Hacker, P. M. S. (2015). Forms of life. (Special Issue 'Wittgenstein and forms of life) *Nordic Wittgenstein Review*, 4:1–20.
Hallet, G. (1977). *A companion to Wittgenstein's philosophical investigations*. Ithica: Cornell University Press.
Hamilton, K. (2001). Wittgenstein's and the mind's eye. In James C. Klagge (Ed.), *Wittgenstein. Biography and philosophy* (pp. 53–97). Cambridge: Cambridge University Press.

Klagge, J. C. (Ed.). (2001). *Wittgenstein. Biography and philosophy*. Cambridge: Cambridge University Press.

Levi, A. W. (1978–79). The sources of Wittgenstein's ethics. *Telos 38* (Winter).

Lyotard, J.-F. (1984). *The postmodern condition: A report on knowledge* (G. Benninton & B. Massumi, Trans.). Minneapolis: University of Minnesota Press. [*La Condition postmoderne: Rapport sur le savoir*. Paris: Éditions de Minuit, 1979.]

Macmillan, C. J. B. (1995). How not to learn: Reflections on Wittgenstein and learning. In J. Marshall & P. Smeyers (Eds.), *Philosophy and education: Accepting Wittgenstein's challenge*. Dordrecht, Boston and London: Kluwer Academic Publishers.

Maruyama, Y. (2017). Elucidation in the transition of Wittgenstein's philosophy. In M. A. Peters & J. Stickney (Eds.), *A companion to Wittgenstein on education: Pedagogical investigations* (pp. 115–121). Singapore: Springer Nature.

McGuinness, B. (1988). *Wittgenstein: A life: Young Ludwig, 1889–1921* (Vol. 1). Los Angeles: University of California Press.

McGuinness, B. (Ed.) (2012) *Wittgenstein in Cambridge: Letters and documents* (4th ed., pp. 1911–1951). Oxford: Wiley-Blackwell.

Magnus, B. (1989). Nietzsche and the postmodern condition. *Nietzsche-Studien, 18*(1), 301.

Malcolm, N. (1981). Wittgenstein's confessions. *London Review of Books, 3* (21) (19 November).

Marshall, J. (1995). Wittgenstein and Foucault: Resolving philosophical puzzles. In J. Marshall & P. Smeyers (Eds.), *Philosophy and education: Accepting Wittgenstein's challenge*. Dordrecht, Boston and London: Kluwer Academic Publishers.

Medina, J. (2002). *The unity of Wittgenstein's philosophy. Necessity, intelligibility, and normativity*. Albany: State University of New York Press.

Monk, R. (1990). *Ludwig Wittgenstein: The duty of genius*. London: Cape.

Monk, R. (1991). *Ludwig Wittgenstein: The duty of genius*. London: Penguin Books.

Monk, R. (2001). Philosophical biography: The very idea. In James C. Klagge (Ed.), *Wittgenstein. Biography and philosophy* (pp. 3–16). Cambridge: Cambridge University Press.

Moore, G. E. (1967). From Wittgenstein's lectures in 1930–33. In K. T. Fann (Ed.), *Ludwig Wittgenstein: The man and his philosophy*. New York: Dell (Also, New Jersey: Humanities Press; and, Sussex: Harvester Press).

Moyal-Sharrock, D. (Ed.). (2004). *The third Wittgenstein*. Oxford: Basil Blackwell.

Nietzsche, F. (1966). *Thus spake Zarathustra* (W. Kaufmann, Trans.). New York: Viking Press.

Oberdan, T. (2013). Moritz Schlick. *Stanford encyclopedia of philosophy*. https://plato.stanford.edu/entries/schlick/.

Peters, M. A. (2001). Philosophy as pedagogy: Wittgenstein's styles of thinking. *Radical Pedagogy*, 3:3. http://radicalpedagogy.icaap.org/content/issue3_3/4-peters.html#1.

Peters, M. A. (2002). Writing the self: Wittgenstein, confession and pedagogy. *Journal of Philosophy of Education, 34*(2), 353–368.

Peters, M. A. (2017). Wittgenstein's trials, teaching and Cavell's romantic "Figure of the Child". In M. A. Peters & J. Stickney (Eds.), *A companion to Wittgenstein on education: Pedagogical investigations* (pp. 211–230). Singapore: Springer.

Peters, M. A., & Marshall, J. (1999). *Wittgenstein: Philosophy, postmodernism, pedagogy*. Westport, CT and London: Bergin and Garvey.

Peters, M. A., Burbules, N., & Smeyers, P. (2008). *Showing and doing: Wittgenstein as a pedagogical philosopher*. London: Routledge.

Quinn, P. (2017). The learner as teacher. In M. A. Peters & J. Stickney (Eds.), *A companion to Wittgenstein on education: Pedagogical investigations* (pp. 703–714). Singapore: Springer.

Rejali, D. (2017). Wittgenstein's hut. In M. A. Peters & J. Stickney (Eds.), *A companion to Wittgenstein on education: Pedagogical investigations* (pp. 79–100). Singapore: Springer Nature.

Rhees, R. (Ed.). (1981). *Ludwig Wittgenstein: Personal recollections*. Oxford: Blackwell.

Rider, S. (2017). Language and mathematical formation. In M. A. Peters & J. Stickney (Eds.), *A companion to Wittgenstein on education: Pedagogical investigations* (pp. 503–516). Singapore: Springer.

Rosenman, S., & Nasti, J. (2012). Psychiatric diagnoses are not mental processes: Wittgenstein on conceptual confusion. *Australian and New Zealand Journal of Psychiatry, 46*(11), 1046–1052.

Savickey, B. (1999). *Wittgenstein's art of investigation*. London and New York: Routledge.

Savickey, B. (2017). Wittgenstein's philosophy: Viva voce. In M. A. Peters & J. Stickney (Eds.), *A companion to Wittgenstein on education: Pedagogical investigations* (pp. 63–78). Singapore: Springer.

Smith, R. D. (2017). Slow learning and the multiplicity of meaning. In M. A. Peters & J. Stickney (Eds.), *A companion to Wittgenstein on education: Pedagogical investigations* (pp. 101–113). Singapore: Springer.

Stickney, J. (2008). Wittgenstein's 'relativity': Agreement in *forms of life* and training in language-games. N. In Burbules & P. Smeyers (guest eds.), M. A. Peters, (ed.). Special Edition on Wittgenstein (September), *Educational Philosophy and Theory, 40*(5).

Stickney, J. (2017). Wittgenstein and judging the soundness of curriculum reforms: Investigating the math wars. In M. A. Peters & J. Stickney (Eds.), *A companion to Wittgenstein on education: Pedagogical investigations* (pp. 481–502). Singapore: Springer.

Von Wright, G. H. (1969). Special supplement: The Wittgenstein papers. *The Philosophical Review, 78*(4), 483–503).

Von Wright, G. H. (1982). Ludwig Wittgenstein: A biographical sketch. In: *Wittgenstein* (pp. 13–34). Oxford: Basil Blackwell.

Williams, M. (1999). *Wittgenstein, mind and meaning. Toward a social conception of mind.* Routledge: London & New York.

Williams, M. (2002). *Wittgenstein, mind and meaning: Towards a social conception of mind.* London: Routledge.

Wittgenstein, H. (1984). My brother Ludwig. In R. Rhees (Ed.), *Recollections of Wittgenstein.* Oxford and New York: Oxford University Press.

Wittgenstein, L. (1956). *Remarks on the foundation of mathematics* (G. E. M. Anscombe, Trans.). Oxford: Basil Blackwell (RFM).

Wittgenstein, L. (1961). *Tractatus Logico-Philosophicus* (D. F. Pears & B. F. McGuinness, Trans.). London: Routledge and Kegan Paul (TLP).

Wittgenstein, L. (1961). *Notebooks 1914–1916* (G. E. M. Anscombe, Trans.). Harper: New York (N).

Wittgenstein, L. (1963). *Philosophical investigations* (G. E. M. Anscombe, Trans.). Oxford: Basil Blackwell (PI).

Wittgenstein, L. (1966). In C. Barrett (Ed.) *Lectures & conversations on aesthetics, psychology and religious beliefs*. Berkeley and London: University of California Press (LC).

Wittgenstein, L. (1967). In G. E. M. Anscombe & G. H. von Wright (Eds.), *Zettel* (G. E. M. Anscombe, Trans.). Oxford: Blackwell (Z).

Wittgenstein, L. (1969). *The blue and brown books: Preliminary studies for the 'Philosophical Investigations'*. Oxford: Basil Blackwell (BB).

Wittgenstein, L. (1974). In R. Rhees (Ed.), *Philosophical grammar* (A. Kenny, Trans.). Oxford: Blackwell (PG).

Wittgenstein, L. (1974). *Letters to Russell, Keynes and Moore* (G. H. von Wright assisted by B. F. McGuinness, Eds.). Oxford: Basil Blackwell (LRKM).

Wittgenstein, L. (1979). In A. Ambrose (Ed.), *Wittgenstein's lectures, Cambridge* (pp. 1932–1935). Oxford: Blackwell (CL).

Wittgenstein, L. (1979). *Ludwig Wittgenstein and the Vienna Circle: Conversations recorded by Friedrich Waismann* (B. McGuinness & J. Schulte, Trans.). New York: Barnes & Noble Books (LWVC).

Wittgenstein, L. (1979). In G. E. M. Anscombe & G. H. von Wright (Eds.), *On certainty* (D. Paul & G. E. M. Anscombe, Trans). Oxford: Basil Blackwell (OC).

Wittgenstein, L. (1980). *Culture and value.* G. H. von Wright (Ed.) in collaboration with H. Nyman. P. Winch (Trans.). Oxford: Basil Blackwell (CV).

Wittgenstein, L. (1993). Lecture on ethics. In J. C. Klagge & A. Nordmann (Eds.), *Philosophical occasions (1912–1951)* (pp. 37–44). Indianapolis and Cambridge: Hackett. (PO: LE)

Wittgenstein, L. (1993). Philosophy. In J. C. Klagge & A. Nordmann (Eds.), *Philosophical occasions (1912–1951)* (pp. 160–199). Indianapolis and Cambridge: Hackett. (PO: Phil.)

Wittgenstein, L. (2000). *Wittgenstein's nachlass. The Bergen electronic edition.* Wittgenstein Archives at the University of Bergen (WAB) and Oxford University Press. http://wab.uib.no/transform/wab.php?modus=opsjoner (WN).

# Chapter 2
# Judging Portraits of Wittgenstein

> We must begin with the mistake and transform it into what is true. That is, we must uncover the source of the error; otherwise hearing what is true won't help us. It cannot penetrate when something is taking its place. To convince someone of what is true, it is not enough to state it; we must find the *road* from error to truth. (RFGB 119)[1]

## 2.1 Introduction

Building on Monk's (2001, 5) analogy of art connoisseurs using expert judgment to determine the suitability of biographical portraiture, we turn to two examples where even good scholars have produced distorted images of Wittgenstein. At risk of reinforcing misimpressions, we correct these caricatures in order to provide a clearer picture of the thinker and his profound relevance to education. Playing with error in this way, we perform *ludic deconstruction* of interpretations in order to bring into focus a more nuanced reading of Wittgenstein.[2]

Wittgenstein's frequent depiction of pedagogical scenes—increasingly prominent in his later writing and in the secondary literature surrounding it (see Marshall 1995; Macmillan 1995; Savickey 1999; Williams 2010; Medina 2002)—naturally

---

[1]Following convention, titles for Wittgenstein's works are abbreviated (PI = Philosophical Investigations, RFM = Remarks on the Foundation of Mathematics, OC = On Certainty, WL = Wittgenstein's Lectures, CV = Culture Value, PO = Philosophical Occasions), with section (§) or page number (p.), with full citation and initials (e.g. RFM) in the References. See Abbreviation list, p. ii?

[2]Compare Wittgenstein (RFGB 119, above) to Goethe's *Wilhelm Meister's Apprenticeship*:

> Not to keep from error, is the duty of the educator of men, but to guide the erring one, even to let him swill his error out of full cups – that is the wisdom of teachers. Whoever merely tastes of his error will keep house with it a long time…but whoever drains it completely will have to get to know it unless he be insane. (von Goethe 2001, VII. 9; Kaufmann 1966, 156)



M. A. Peters and J. Stickney, *Wittgenstein's Education: 'A Picture Held Us Captive'*, SpringerBriefs on Key Thinkers in Education
https://doi.org/10.1007/978-981-10-8411-9_2

strikes interest among academics working within education. Instead of extracting a theory of pedagogy from these vignettes, in Chaps. 3 and 4, we seek to offer a synoptic view of the role teaching and learning examples play in Wittgenstein's later philosophic method: seeing them as a 'pedagogical way of doing philosophy' (see Peters and Marshall 1999, 174–5). Sage advice is not to look for educational theory in Wittgenstein's writing but to see his later philosophy *as* pedagogical (Peters 1995; Peters and Marshall 1999; Stickney 2005; Peters et al. 2008/2010), or, as therapeutic (Standish et al. 2007). As Glock (1996, 111–2) explains, in his later philosophy Wittgenstein attends to how words are taught not to 'engage in armchair learning-theory' or to offer any 'empirical genetic theory', but to show conceptually that teaching by explanation presupposes basic linguistic skills we are not born with, but acquire by means of training. Early training into shared practices or techniques provides a (non-rationalist) foundation for judging whether a pupil is following the teacher's explanations, or clearly understands how to go on as intended in the lessons.

For philosophers of education, Wittgenstein's remarks pose the challenge of not fetishizing references to educational terms: 'teach', 'learn', 'train', 'education' and 'pupil' draw educationists in when reading these scenes, partly obscuring their philosophical significance.

> A poet's words can pierce us. And this is of course causally connected with the use that they have in our life. And it also is connected with the way in which, comfortable to this use, we let our thoughts roam up and down in the familiar surroundings of the words. (Z §155)[3]

Realizing that words we dwell on can strike, Wittgenstein counsels Stoic calmness (*ataraxia*):

> My ideal is a certain coolness, a temple providing a setting for the passions without meddling with them. (CV 2e)

Characteristic of Wittgenstein is the desire, though usually frustrated by his own tortured prose, to write philosophy as though composing music or writing poetry.

> I think I summed up my attitude to philosophy when I said: Philosophy ought really to be written only as *poetic composition*. It must, as it seems to me, be possible to gather from this how far my thinking belongs to the present, future or past. For I was thereby revealing myself as someone who cannot do what he would like to be able to do. (CV 24e)

[3]Reacting to someone exhibiting pain behaviour is similar: we have grown accustomed to readings these gestures and sounds, and recognize them instantly without making elaborate inferences, because we have been surrounded by these patterns and rituals of reaction all of our lives.

> Only surrounded by certain normal manifestations of life is there such a thing as an expression of pain. Only surrounded by an even more far-reaching particular manifestation of life, such a thing as the expression of sorrow or affection. And so on. (Z §534)

## 2.2 Geographical Digressions: A Parable on Finding Our Way Back Home

> /Teaching philosophy involves the same immense difficulty as instruction in geography would have if a pupil brought with him a mass of false and far too simple // and falsely simplified // ideas about the course and connections of the routes of rivers // rivers // and mountain chains // mountains//./ (PO, Phil., 185)

Sometimes comparative cases show a problem in relief, as though looking in from the outside. Before residing within academic Philosophy of Education, both authors (Peters and Stickney) taught Geography in high schools. Perhaps this background predisposes us to find affinity with Wittgenstein's writing, as he frequently uses geographical metaphors in conveying his philosophy, and even likens teaching philosophy to teaching geography—something in which Wittgenstein participated, in the classroom and even taking his elementary students on trips to Vienna. But therein lies the danger, as the tendency is to read the analogy with feelings of kinship or ownership. For instance, Michael Curry (2000, 110) wrote that Wittgenstein's 'work has something more to say directly to geographers'. Countering the tendency among academic geographers to overlook the relevance of Wittgenstein's philosophy (as perhaps too obtuse or remote), Curry (2000, 90) made a greatly inflated, proprietary claim:

> It seems to me, quite to the contrary, that Wittgenstein might be seen as *the* geographical philosopher. Indeed, …Wittgenstein has been the philosopher whose work has most deeply and dramatically addressed problems that have exercised geographers. And he has addressed these problems—of the role of space in philosophy, social theory, and common sense; of the importance of places; and of the nature of the natural—in a truly radical way, in a way that gets at the root of the matter.

Curry's point was that 'right at the heart' of Wittgenstein's work 'is a deep appreciation of places and their role in everyday lives', adding that Wittgenstein somehow 'cuts through the welter of spatial metaphors in which we live' (110). As Wittgenstein scholars and geographers these descriptions confound us, though in fairness they do not seem characteristic of Curry's other achievements or stature as an academic. Philosopher of Geography Joseph May (deceased),[4] who is one of the few to have written a monograph on Wittgenstein's use of spatial metaphors, would never have elevated Wittgenstein's significance for the discipline of Geography above a philosopher like Kant, who actually taught extensively and wrote on the subject of Geography and for whom 'space' figured prominently in his thinking (May 1970; cf. Elden 2011). At most, Wittgenstein is said to have had a globe in his

[4]May was Stickney's MA thesis advisor at University of Toronto. Having done his BA at University of Minnesota, Stickney visited with Curry there when he was completing his MA Thesis, 'Forms of life: A Wittgensteinian view' (Wittgenstein 1980a, b). (See also Curry 1989.)

elementary classroom and did indeed occasionally ponder how we perceive things in space (e.g. a brown book sitting on a table before us),[5] as epistemological matters or remarks on the philosophy of psychology. Kant's lectures on geography, on the other hand, were among his most well attended at the University of Königsburg, and he left behind detailed lectures notes on Physical Geography (Elden 2011).

Having seen how a geographical appropriation can go astray, let's now look at how Wittgenstein actually referred to places: serving both as an introduction to a central tenet of his philosophy (meaning-as-use) and as a parallel case to the ways in which educators receive Wittgenstein's references to 'training', 'teaching', 'learning' and 'pupils'. In the Preface to the *Philosophical Investigations*, he describes his book as an album of landscape sketches:

> After several unsuccessful attempts to weld my results together into such a whole, I realized that I should never succeed. The best that I could write would never be more than philosophical remarks; my thoughts were soon crippled if I tried to force them on in any single direction against their natural inclination.—And this was, of course, connected with the very nature of the investigation. For this compels us to travel over a wide field of thought criss-cross in every direction.—The philosophical remarks in this book are, as it were, a number of sketches of landscapes which were made in the course of these long and involved journeyings.
>
> The same or almost the same points were always being approached afresh from different directions, and new sketches made. Very many of these were badly drawn or uncharacteristic, marked by all the defects of a weak draughtsman. And when they were rejected a number of tolerable ones were left, which now had to be arranged and sometimes cut down, so that if you looked at them you could get a picture of the landscape. Thus this book is really only an album. (PI, p. ix)

These opening remarks clearly address the problems he experienced as an author with his composition,[6] and in the absence of a more rigorous method provide a way of looking at his remarks, as though ambling through space and happening upon the same place several times from different vantage points. Sometimes you 'approach from *one* side and you know your way about; you approach the same place from another side and no longer know your way about' (PI §203). The idea is repeated in other remarks on his 'method', a word we use carefully as it conveys the original

[5]The concept of 'seeing' makes a tangled impression. Well, it is tangled—I look at the landscape, my gaze ranges over it, I see all sorts of distinct and indistinct movement; *this* impresses itself sharply on me, *that* [it] is quite hazy. After all, how completely ragged what we see can appear! And now look at all that can be meant by 'description of what is seen'—But this just is what is called description of what is seen. There is not *one genuine* proper case of such description—the rest being just vague, something which awaits clarification, or which must be swept aside as rubbish (PI, pg. 200; Cf. PI 291, 292).

[6]'Here I am inclined to fight windmills, because I cannot yet say the thing I really want to say.' (OC §400)

sense of a *meta-ton-hodos* or 'procession along a path'—here depicted topographically as traversing a countryside or winding through crowded city streets.[7]

> I am trying to conduct you on tours in a certain country. I will try to show that the philosophical difficulties which arise in mathematics as elsewhere arise because we find ourselves in a strange town and do not know our way. So we must learn the topography by going from one place in the town to another, and from there to another, and so on. And one must do this so often that one knows one's way, either immediately or pretty soon after looking around a bit, wherever one may be set down." (LFM, 44; see Ch 1 for a similar passage in Gasking and Jackson's chapter, "Wittgenstein as a teacher," 1967, 52)

> I am showing my pupils details of an immense landscape which they cannot possibly know their way around. (CV 56e)

On another level, however, he also wants us to see language itself as though a bounded space, and most easily as a city in which we reside. The metaphor is rich in also allowing us to see musical or math notation as suburbs of language, and beyond these frontiers the realm of the ineffable.

> Our language can be seen as an ancient city: a maze of little streets and squares, of old and new houses, and of houses with additions from various periods; and this surrounded by a multitude of new boroughs with straight regular streets and uniform houses. (PI §18)

This spatial thinking is not a new development, as in the *Tractatus* he concluded that, 'The limits of my language mean the limits of my world' (TLP 5.6). In his 'Lecture on Ethics' (see Ch 1), he compares the honourable attempt to state things such as the goal in life, or precepts of right conduct as 'running up against the boundaries of language', which recalls an ancient sentiment from Lao Tzu on the failure of words to capture the cosmic breadth of the Tao—the meaning or 'path' of life.

Wittgenstein's later concept of 'philosophy' is most explicitly spatial, as is his description of the central task in philosophy of helping us stay within the boundaries of sense, guiding us away from flights into metaphysical fancy:

> A philosophical problem has the form: "I don't know my way about." (PI §123)

> For philosophical problems arise when language *goes on holiday*. (PI §38).

Where is it we need to orient ourselves? Within the boundaries of sensible language, or along the paths set down for us by our cultural tradition that dictate ordinary usage and common sense (see Gasparatou 2017).

---

[7]In PI, p. 225 Wittgenstein demonstrates *mastery of techniques* through gradual training as follows, discussing how one is able to judge the length of rod (for allusion to Einstein's relativity, see Stickney 2008): 'What "determining the length" means is not learned by learning what *length* and *determining* are; the meaning not the word "length" is learnt by learning, among other things, what it is to determine length.

(For this reason the word "methodology" has a double meaning. Not only a physical investigation, but also a conceptual one, can be called "methodical investigation".)'

> …In the actual use of expressions we make detours, we go by side-roads. We see the straight highway before us, but of course we cannot use it, because it is permanently closed. (PI §426)

Instead of the 'crystalline purity' of logic he sought by means of a ladder in his *Tractatus* (see Ch 1), in his *Investigations* he takes us on the downward path, 'back to the rough ground' (PI §107).[8]

To think that Wittgenstein is talking about geography here is to contort his philosophical prose, committing what Ryle (after Wittgenstein) called a 'category mistake' (see also Ryle 1949, 323 and 327 for geographic metaphors). Wittgenstein's spatial metaphors bring home the warning not to stray, as when we try to offer an 'bewitching' explanation when an apt depiction would suffice (PI §109). The reason we so often get lost has much to do with the labyrinthine nature of language itself, and how it had grown at places hazardous over the long period of time that constitutes both our natural and social history (see PI §26, and PI, p. 230).

> /People are deeply imbedded in philosophical, i.e. grammatical confusions. And to free them from these presupposes pulling them out of the immensely manifold connections they are caught up in. One must so to speak regroup their entire language. – But this language came about // developed // as it did because human beings had – and have – the tendency to think in this way. So you can only succeed in extricating people who live in an instinctive rebellion against // dissatisfaction with // language. Not with those who following all their instincts live within the herd that has created this language as its proper expression. (PO 185)

The Nietzschean sentiment of breaking with the herd is part of his exhortation to philosophy, as a guide from linguistic entrapment.

> Where do // did / the old philosophical problems get their importance from? (PO 169)
>
> Above all, our grammar is lacking in perspicuity. (PO 177)
>
> Language contains the same traps for everyone; the immense network of well-kept // passable // false paths. (PO 185)

Wittgenstein addresses this problem in grappling with continued talk of the 'river of time', a phrase originating in Heraclitus' aphorism that 'everything is in flux' (*panta rhei*).

> Language cannot express what belongs to the essence of the world. Therefore it cannot say that everything flows. Language can only say what we could also imagine differently.
>
> That everything flows must lie in how language touches reality. Or better: that everything flows must lie in the nature of language. And let's remember: in everyday life we don't notice that – as little as we notice the blurred edges of our visual field ("because we are so used to it", some will say). How, on what occasion, do we think we start noticing it? Isn't it when we want to form sentences in opposition to the grammar of time? *Philosophy,* (PO 188)

---

[8]'The more narrowly we examine actual language, the sharper becomes the conflict between it and our requirement. (For the crystalline purity of logic was, of course, not a result of investigation: it was a requirement.) The conflict becomes intolerable; the requirement is now in danger of becoming empty—We have go onto slippery ice where there is no friction and so in a certain sense the conditions are ideal, but also, just because of that, we are unable to walk. We want to walk: so we need friction. Back to the rough ground!' (PI §107).

In talking about the 'fluidity of all things over time', we hazard down one of the dead-ends of philosophical thinking (*aporia*) that Rorty (1979)—who popularized in the 1970s the phrase 'the linguistic turn in philosophy'—wisely cautioned us to aver.

> People say again and again that philosophy doesn't really progress, that we are still occupied with the same philosophical problems as were the Greeks. But the people who say this don't understand why it is has to be so. It is because our language has remained the same and keeps seducing us into asking the same questions. As long as there continues to be a verb 'to be' that looks as if it functions in the same way as 'to eat' and 'to drink', as long as we still have the adjectives 'identical', 'true', 'false', 'possible', as long as we continue to talk of a river of time, of an expanse of space, etc., etc., people will keep stumbling over the same puzzling difficulties and find themselves staring at something which no explanation seems capable of clearing up.
>
> And what's more, this satisfies a longing for the transcendent, because in so far as people think they can see the "limits of human understanding", they believe of course that they can see beyond these. (CV 15e)

Our language is haunted, we might say, by its legacy of prior grammatical development and usage—its baggage of concepts and metaphors that have concretized into its very bedrock (OC §§94–98).[9]

> Concepts lead us to make investigations: are the expressions of our interest, and direct our interest. (PI §570)[10]

Words, as he depicts them, are charged with 'fields of force' (PI, p. 219) and may even harbour 'souls', (PI §§530–32; cf. §§219–19) giving us play-space to make fine aesthetic distinctions. To understand expressions, meaningfully-in-use (PI §43), we need to traverse their local 'haunts' or 'ranges' (*ethos*; see Heidegger and Fink 1970), at times finding irreplaceable words or gestures around emotional expressions by surveying their 'atmospheres' or 'circumstances' (Z §534).

With this freedom and constraint within the connotative range and grammar of words comes the uncanny realization that our conventional meanings and criteria for correct usage can be overwhelmed. Cavell (2005) astutely notes that 'the *Investigations* portrays our lives (with their little outbreaks of madness) as

---

[9]OC §95; 'It might be imagined that some propositions, of the form of empirical propositions, were hardened and functioned as channels for such propositions as were not hardened but fluid; and that this relation altered with time, in that fluid propositions hardened, and hard ones became fluid.' OC §96; 'The mythology may change back into a state of flux, the river-bed of thoughts may shift. But I distinguish between the movement of the waters on the river-bed and the shift of the bed itself; though there is not a sharp division of one from then other.' OC §97; 'And the bank of that river consists partly of hard rock, subject to no alteration or only to an imperceptible one, partly of sand, which now in one place now in another gets washed away, or deposited.' (OC §99)

[10]Would it be correct to say that our concepts reflect our life? They stand in the middle of it. (RC III, §302)

You have a new conception and interpret it as seeing a new object. You interpret a grammatical movement made by yourself as a quasi-physical phenomenon which you are observing. ...What you primarily discovered was a new way of looking at things. (OC §401)

something extraordinary, strange, in a sense unnatural', connecting this estrangement with 'our cursed and blessed capacity for adaptation and conformity'.

> To possess criteria is also to possess the demonic power to strip them from ourselves, to turn language upon itself, to find that its criteria are, in relation to others, merely outer; in relation to certainty, simply blind; in relation to being able to go on with our concepts into new contexts, wholly ungrounded. (Cavell 2005, 205, citing his earlier book, *The Claim of Reason*)
>
> So how are we to understand what presents itself in the *Investigations* as our drive to senselessness, our demonic threat to carry ourselves away? (Cavell 2005, 207)

In epic fashion, Cavell's description of our relationship to language entails perilous venturing away and nostalgic return. The Heraclitean and Pindaric formula for 'searching ourselves' and 'becoming who we are' is found in Wittgenstein's search for 'knowing our way about'—for coming home to a lost order we have forgotten was there, operating out of reach of our 'eyes and ears' but pervading the world as we know it, as meaningful and navigable within human limits.

> In this sequence of thoughts about the ordinary, each way in which, in philosophizing, we come upon ourselves denying our human powers produces a clause in an open-ended mythological description of our everyday lives – as exile, or making ourselves strange to ourselves, or constructing unsatisfying substitutes for a fantasied lost harmony, or violently asserting a singularity guaranteed by metaphysics rather than making our words and deeds our own: … (Cavell 2005, 201)

Wittgenstein's authenticity rhetoric has the markings of therapeutic 'homecoming', invoking the humility of wearing 'homespun' clothing.

> What we do is to bring words back from their metaphysical to their correct use in language.
>
> (The man who said that one cannot step into the same river twice said something wrong; one can step into the same river twice.)
>
> And this is what the solution of all philosophical difficulties looks like. Their answers, if they are correct, must be *homespun* and *ordinary*. But one must look at them in the proper spirit, and *then it doesn't matter*. (PO 167–9; cf. 188)

Cavell (2005, 201) finds in this philosophical prose a 'mythology of the ordinary' that 'produces the sense of a continuing effort to recognize the extraordinariness with the ordinariness of our lives'. Wittgenstein conveys this rather phenomenological theme in the following passage:

> The aspects of things that are most important for us are hidden because of their simplicity and familiarity. (One is unable to notice something – because it is always before one's eyes.) The real foundations of his inquiry do not strike a man at all. Unless *that* fact has at some time struck him. – And this means: we feel to be struck by what, once seen, is most striking and most powerful. (PI §129) [11]

[11]Gadamer (1977, 176), says of this sentence: "And what would be nearer to the later Husserl and his interest in the life-world or to Heidegger's analytic of everyday Dasein than this sentence …") (citing PI §129 above).

Addressing this strange sense of the extraordinary amidst the ordinary, Cavell notes parenthetically (202):

> (And yet this capacity can be nothing other than, must deploy the same powers and constraints as, our capacity for transformation, for, in the Romantic formula, becoming the one who you are – so that the path of a human life is the resultant of these contrary powers.)

How are we to find our way home? Wittgenstein's deep contextualism, as well as his post-foundational epistemology, is expressed in Heraclitean terms of finding temporary bedrock within the shifting stream of life (OC §§94–99).

> Conversation, the application and interpretation of words flows on, and only in the *flow* of life does a word have its meaning. (Z §135)

> Words only have meaning in the river of thought and life. (Z §174; cf. §173)[12]

The stabilizing guide within this 'flux', whether for rule-following or comprehension, is found outside us in the social milieu or cultural background, against which we see (picture) and judge actions and into which we passively and actively introduce our young.

> We judge an action according to its background within human life, and this background is not monochrome, but we might picture it as a very complicated filigree pattern, which, to be sure, we can't copy, but which we can recognize from the general impression it makes. (RPP II, §624)

> How could human behavior be described? Surely only by sketching the actions of a variety of humans, as they are all mixed up together. What determines our judgement, our concepts and reactions, is not what one man is doing now, an individual action, but the whole hurly-burly of human actions, the background against which we see any action. (Z §567)

> What determines our judgment, our concepts and reactions, is not what one man is doing now, an individual action, but the whole hurly-burly of human actions, the background against which we see any action.

> Seeing life as a weave, this pattern (pretence, say) is not always complete and is varied in a multiplicity of ways... And one pattern in the weave is interwoven with many others. (Z §§567–69; cf. RPP II, §§626–629)

Although part of our 'education' in its broadest sense, the needed background for comprehension is not easily conveyed through direct instruction; it is imparted gradually, however, through initiate training and experience—like weighing imponderable evidence for sensing emotions on the face (PI, p. 227–8) or gaining a nose for good coffee (PI, p. 218). As we see in the next section, appreciation of this gradual and often informal enculturation process is lacking in Friesen's assault on Wittgenstein's frequent reference to 'training'.

---

[12]"There's some behaviour and some conversation taking place. A few sentences back and forth; and a few actions. That might be all. (Words only have meaning in the river [Flux] of life.) (LW, I §913)

> I do not explicitly learn the propositions that stand fast for me. I can *discover* them subsequently like the axis around which a body rotates. This axis is not fixed in the sense that anything holds it fast, but the movement around it determines its immobility. (OC §152)

Coming 'home' to our familiar ground in language is conveyed in terms of taking up a stance in common with others, as though joining them in the public square or around a May pole: people with whom we can 'find our feet' (PI §223) sharing a *form of life* or 'agreements in judgment' (PI §§241–2). If someone speaks nonsense about 'earth-born cars', we let this drift away: never cohering or sedimenting into our common bedrock.

> It is quite sure that motorcars don't grow out of the earth. We feel if someone could believe the contrary he could believe *everything* that we say is untrue, and could question everything that we hold to be sure.
>
> But how does this *one* belief hang together with all the rest? We should like to say that someone who could believe that does not accept our whole system of verification.
>
> This system is something a human being acquires by means of observation and instruction. I intentionally do not say "learns". (OC §279)
>
> After he has seen this and this and heard that and that, he is not in a position to doubt whether… (OC §280)

In OC §281, he stresses that one who does not *agree* with what we hear, read and experience seems mad to us—as though they do not share the common basis of *agreement*. In OC §282, he stresses that one could only doubt whether he had parents if he had been *taught* that from the beginning.[13]

> For how can a child immediately doubt what it is taught? That could mean only that he was incapable of learning certain language-games. (OC §283)

In Wittgenstein's 'mythology of the ordinary'[14], our common surroundings (*circs*) play the role of the *genius loci*[15]: a living, grammatical or social context guiding us toward shared but always fragile senses of certainty in linguistic practice, knowledge and judgment. Speaking of this inherited background, he wrote:

[13]In OC §286: What we believe depends on what we learn. (See OC §§310–15, cited below.)

[14]Built upon Heidegger's *spatialization* of language; see Heidegger and Fink (1970), Heidegger (1977a, b).

[15]Instead of Nietzsche's (1965, 129) and Emerson's (1965, 294, 300, 305–6) familiar trope of a singular tutelary spirit or 'daimon'.

> There can be no more detestable and empty creature in nature than the man who runs away from his *daimon*, and then casts furtive glances right, left, backwards and all around. One can no longer seize hold of such a man, for he is all exterior without any core, a decrepit, painted, puffed up garment, an ornate ghost which can inspire no fear and certainly no sympathy. (Nietzsche 1965, 2–3)

> Now it gives our way of looking at things, and our researches, their form. Perhaps it was once disputed. But perhaps for unthinkable ages, it has belonged to the *scaffolding* of our thoughts. (Every human being has parents.) (OC §211)

Attending to circumstances or surroundings (as with words but also gestures, expressions or math symbols, music notation, etc.) also sets the stage for reading Wittgenstein many 'scenes of instruction', in which we encounter students who 'doubt too much' or 'go against rules', inviting us to appropriate or reject their instances of remarkable Otherness (see OC §§279–283; see Ch 1).

> But I did not get my picture of the world by satisfying myself of its correctness; nor do I have it because I am satisfied of its correctness. No: it is the inherited background against which I distinguish between true and false. (OC §94; cf. §140 and 152)

## 2.3 Replacing a Distorted Portrait of 'Training' in the Later Wittgenstein: Why Does the Training Word, *Abrichtung*, Pierce Educators?[16]

### *2.3.1 Stage Setting*

Investigating geographic metaphors in Wittgenstein's philosophical prose (see Burbules 2017), we considered the 'atmospheres' of words, arriving at the realization that the way we 'let our thoughts roam up and down in the familiar surroundings of the words' allows '[a poet's] words to pierce us' (Z §155). Here, we make the case that something similar is happening among some interpreters of Wittgenstein within education, as they overreact to his use of the German word *abrichtung*: a word often reserved in the vernacular for harsh forms of 'animal training' or 'conditioning' but translated as 'training' by Elizabeth Anscombe in the *Philosophical Investigations* (see Ch 1). At the outset of Kant's *Pedagogy* (§6, 106), he distinguishes two sources of education for humans: 'Man needs care and education. Training and instruction are included under education.' Animals, on the other hand, do not require such training (§3, 102), with the possible exception of birds learning songs: 'Discipline, or training, changes animal nature into human nature. An animal is already fully equipped', he says, through instinct. In keeping with his deontological view of ethics, the pupil must not only be disciplined into doing the right thing (passively or bodily obeying) but must fully appreciate (actively or mentally) the rule or maxim upon which moral duty is founded (§§70–71; cf. §§77, 78). The paradox that we train pupils toward rational autonomy (as opposed to heteronomy) was developed by Kant into an antinomy:

---

[16]A portion of this section was presented at the *Philosophy of Education Society of Great Britain* annual meeting (Oxford 2018).

> One of the greatest problems in education is, How can subjection to lawful constraint be combined with the ability to make use of one's freedom? For constraint is necessary. How shall I cultivate freedom under conditions of compulsion? I ought to accustom my pupil to tolerate a restraint upon his freedom, and at the same time lead him to make good use of his freedom. (Kant 1904, §29, p. 131)

For Kant, the 'training' issue is rooted in his father's strict Pietism, with deep roots in Lutheran thought about moral 'correction', or bringing the pupil into proper 'alignment' with God's purpose and a humbling before the power of the Prussian state—hence 'righted' or *abrichtung*. Wittgenstein's use of the word *abrichtung*, however, cannot be fathomed from such historical inquiry, if we are to heed his admonition to look for *meaning-as-use* as opposed to etymologies and chronicles.[17]

> The historical explanation, the explanation as an hypothesis of development, is only *one* way of assembling the data – of their synopsis. It is just as possible to see the data in their relation to one another and to embrace them in a general picture without putting it in the form of an hypothesis about temporal development. (PO: RFGB 131)

One of the fruits of the analytic tradition in Philosophy of Education—R. S. Peters and Paul Hirst's 1960s usage of Wittgenstein's later work—was the practice of 'concept mapping' by which they distinguished the concept of 'teaching' from terms bearing a 'family resemblance' (cf. PI §§68–70): conditioning, training, advertising, proselytizing, indoctrinating, etc. Unlike its cousins, 'teaching' (they said) involves the weighing of evidence and the giving of reasons—rational or critical dispositions we have come to cherish through the Enlightenment (Locke, Rousseau, Kant, Mill) and the tradition of liberal philosophy (Oakeshott, Rawls) as perquisites for autonomy: mental and civic freedom. Read from this analytic mindset, Wittgenstein's references to *abrichtung* seem to run counter to the liberal tradition.

In the field of Education, we also have the disturbing problem of having to respond to biographical reports on Wittgenstein's use of corporal punishment in his elementary classroom: accusations of pulling girls' hair and cuffing boys ears, which led to his expulsion from teaching (see Bartley 1973). Whether or not Wittgenstein's volatile temperament was related to diagnoses of autism or Asperger's, reading these accounts of an enraged educator (regardless of frequency) is admittedly disappointing. Derek Jarman shows this degenerative tendency in a scene from his movie 'Wittgenstein', in which he ends a session of teaching in his room at Cambridge with a shouting match.[18] Accepting the validity of these various reports, it would be extremely unwise to proceed in writing a hagiographic account of 'Wittgenstein as Educator'.

---

[17]Wittgenstein criticized Fraser for crudely interpreting as sinister rites like Beltane fire festivals where effigies are thrown onto the fire and drawing lots (initially for human sacrifice). We are uncertain of (cannot verify) historical hypotheses, he says, and so must look for something sinister in the present enactment of rituals—'the surroundings of a way of acting'—and ascribe this sense from inner experience (PO: RFGB 147).

[18]https://www.youtube.com/watch?v=r0cN_bpLrxk.

Despite the considerable legacy of work on Wittgenstein in Philosophy of Education, we now find ourselves in an awkward situation: Not trying to exonerate Wittgenstein of all criticism, for the *Key Thinkers in Education* series we are defending his suitability as an inspirational or pivotal thinker in our field. Here, we have to acknowledge the danger in trying to safeguard Wittgenstein's philosophy from accusations of 'brutality': in providing a defence, one risks amplifying or entrenching the very misimpressions one is trying to expunge. Over the last 5 years, Norm Friesen has launched a veritable tribunal (online, at conferences, and in print), basing his indictment of Wittgenstein being a 'tragic philosopher of education' on frequent use of the German word *abrichtung* (translated harshly as 'animal training'). In fairness, he is picking up on a theme on which Michael Luntley has expounded over many years, and which has gained some traction in other fields as well. We find in Luntley, however, a more creative or original interpretation of Wittgenstein, albeit one few share in philosophy and that we reject as it focuses on the individual (the *cogitans*) after Descartes' rationalist philosophy, arguing that there must be something inside the learner that provides the capacity for training to take hold (or, as he puts it, conditioning and response, *plus* something else internal and rational).[19]

As a qualifier, we are not objecting to Friesen's right (academic freedom) to share his views; he in fact published his paper in *Educational Philosophy and Theory,* edited by Michael A. Peters. Nor are we discrediting everything Friesen said in the paper, as he also entertained connections to Janik and Toulmin's (1973) cultural reading of Wittgenstein, and Foucault's reflections on self-constitution that are close to our own interests. We also want to take care not to disparage all of his work in the field nor discourage others from engaging in critical investigations of Wittgenstein. It was refreshing, for instance, to include in our *Companion to Wittgenstein on Education* book Stephen Burwood's critique, questioning whether Wittgenstein in effect supressed independent thinking in his Cambridge seminars (see Burwood 2017; see also Ch 1). As in the case of critiquing Curry's adoption of Wittgenstein to Geography, using a striking caricature gives us occasion to correct the portrait, much as a painting instructor shows where there is need for recomposing the subject in relation to its background, or shifts the emphasis by altering the colour pallet, redirecting strokes of the brush or adding scrapes of the pallet knife.

---

[19]Friesen's fixation on *abrichtung* finds some affinity in the writing of Michael Luntley (2007, 2008, 2012, Luntley 2017, 442), stemming from Huemer's (2006) paper, but Luntley perseveres in seeing in Wittgenstein a source of inspiration for what he calls an *aesthetic sensibility attuned to our innate conditions or capacities for learning*. The Luntley-Stickney debate of 2008 did not go entirely unnoticed in the field of academic Philosophy in which Luntley resides, making a footnote in Andrea Kern's *Sources of Knowledge* (Kern 2017, 666). (See index entries for *abrichtung*, in Peters and Stickney 2017.)

### 2.3.2 *Friesen's Misreading: Reacting Incorrectly to Wittgenstein's Remarks*

After a brief excursus of the opening emphasis on training in the *Investigations* (e.g. PI §§5–6, see below), Friesen builds his case by citing Wittgenstein's statement in the *Preliminary Notebooks* (BB 77), that:

> The child learns this language … by being trained to its use. I am using the word 'trained' in a way strictly analogous to that in which we talk of an animal being trained to do certain things. It is done by means of example, reward, punishment, and such like. (1958, p. 77)

Friesen's (2017, 69) hurried claim is that Wittgenstein is therefore a behaviourist—something Wittgenstein explicitly denies in PI §§307–309 (see Medina 2004, 82–4, in Ch 3)—in seemingly advocating the use of reward and punishment in teaching. We show instead (also in Chaps. 1 and 4) that he was creating a simplified thought-experiment (as he explained in PI §5) to illustrate how children *do* learn their first language through absorption of the background, and not just through more pedantic *ostensive teaching*: acquiring *ostensive definitions* (rich contexts and a grammar of word-use) through enculturation instead of pointing gestures, we might use to anchor names (e.g. '*that,* over there, is a *cat*' presupposes understanding the concepts of 'here' and 'there' as well as the role 'that' plays in ostensive language-games). The context leading up to Wittgenstein's early remark on animal-like training was an observation on how we internalize language without having to explicitly refer to grammatical rules (see BB 25, in Ch 4). Having missed Wittgenstein's early and later descriptions of intent, and the fact that Wittgenstein omitted these remarks on animal training in revising the notebooks into the more polished *Investigations* (see Winch 2018; cf. PI §§1–6 in Ch 1), Friesen continues to stray into gross exaggeration about all of Wittgenstein's later work:

> It is with uncomfortably purposeful and unambiguous characterizations of this kind that problems arise for philosophical interpretations of Wittgenstein's statements on teaching, learning, and education more broadly. For Wittgenstein's insistence on learning (language) through reward and punishment is consistent and systematic, both in the *Philosophical Investigations* and elsewhere.

Responding to Friesen's (2016) presentation at the *Philosophy of Education Society* meeting in Toronto (Friesen 2016), an audience member [Stickney] noted that what had been presented were serial accusations of impropriety or even suggestions of indecency, brought strategically before a 'jury' who would later be instructed to dismiss some of the wilder conjectures and innuendo (e.g. even conjuring images of black leather and homosexual sadomasochism). Used in connection with Bartley's biographical accounts of Wittgenstein's use of corporal punishment in his elementary classroom, the combined effect was to engrain a picture of brutality that the 'jury' could not easily dislodge. In publishing his paper, Friesen (2017, 71) again employs this barrister's technique when he 'acknowledges, but avoids undue speculation on the biographical reality of literal and brutal assaults visited by Wittgenstein as a school teacher on his young charges in the mid-twenties (Monk 1991, pp. 224, 232–233)'.[20] The adjoining footnote (76, #2) reads:

> As a teacher in rural Austria, Wittgenstein regularly pulled the hair and boxed the ears of his pupils, sometimes drawing blood. At one point, he struck a boy on the head with sufficient force to cause him to collapse on the floor, unconscious. Wittgenstein's immediate response was to leave the classroom, the village and also his post as a teacher. Hearings were held at a district court, but the case was suddenly dropped, perhaps through the influence of Wittgenstein's wealthy family.

After parental complaints, Wittgenstein was in fact called to a tribunal over the *Haibauer* incident (1926; see Ch 3 and Peters 2017), but instead of defending himself he chose to leave the teaching profession; he later assumed a chair in philosophy at Cambridge (1929–1947), often reflecting on his teaching experience in delivering poignant illustrations for his later philosophy of language (see Chap. 1).

Combined with select textual evidence, Friesen's case may at first seem compelling. Wittgenstein did connect our learning of pointing gestures to animal training in his 'Preliminary Notebooks' (BB 77), noting that dogs but not cats respond appropriately to the sign, but there is no hint of cruelty in the example as Friesen suggests, crudely using a dictionary definition of *abrichtung* to indicate 'severe treatment'.

> The standard German (*Duden*) Dictionary defines *Abrichtung* as directed toward '(an animal, esp. a dog) to train for particular action and abilities; dressage.' Langenscheidt's German-English dictionary provides two entries for the term: '*(animal)* train;' also, 'teach an animal tricks; *(horse)* break in,' adding these example phrases: to 'train an animal to…' or to 'train a dog to attack people.' The second entry provided for *Abrichten* in Langenscheidt's refers to woodwork or machine work. It identifies the act of 'trueing' something; 'to justify, pare, plane, straighten or level.' (Friesen 2017, 72)

The prosecutor might add, though Friesen overlooked this evidence: 'Doesn't Wittgenstein also admit to Nietzschean views on discipline, referring to the benefits of students developing a 'capacity for suffering (CV 71e)': remarks that appear rather untimely now?

It is too easy here to rush to conviction, and also to disparagement of the careers of so many distinguished scholars working with Wittgenstein's philosophy in education. On his website,[21] including harsh language drafted for his Friesen's

---

[20]Preceded by the concession (emphasis added, 71), though aimed at sidestepping the reading of Wittgenstein's use of *abrichtung* as a rhetorical device: 'This paper argues that it is neither necessary nor helpful to see Wittgenstein's language—*despite its unyielding harshness*—simply as 'inappropriate' or an 'assault' on his readers.' What harshness is he pointing to PI §§207–8, as an example?

[21]Lost in Translation: Ludwig Wittgenstein, Education and the Question of Abrichtung (Training). Posted on 5 August 2015 by friesenn

http://blogs.ubc.ca/nfriesen/2015/08/05/lost-in-translation-ludwig-wittgenstein-education-and-the-question-of-abrichtung-training.

Any cautious, constructive interpretive response to Wittgenstein's startling affirmation of Abrichtung in education—of commanding children as animals, perhaps even to break their will—would have to consider unflinchingly why Wittgenstein deliberately chose such a forceful term in the first place. It would have to ask why Wittgenstein insisted on arbitrary brutality as being

(2017; 2016) paper, Friesen insinuates that Smeyers, Burbules, Peters and Stickney (among others) are duped in using Wittgenstein supposedly for progressive purposes in education. He overlooks their now familiar presentation of Wittgenstein as a 'pedagogical philosopher' (see Chap. 3) instead of a theorist of education (Marshall and Smeyers 1995; Peters and Marshall 1999; Peters et al. 2008).

Taken somewhat aback by the negative reception of his PES paper, Friesen (2017) was only a little more cautious in publishing his critique in *Educational Philosophy and Theory*, where he targeted luminaries in the field: first, Smeyers and Burbules' (2010; cf. Smeyers and Burbules 2005/2006/2010) paper on 'Education as initiation into practices'; and second, Winch's (2002) chapter on training in *The philosophy of human learning*, as examples of blatant disregard for the 'real' meaning of Wittgenstein's references to training, as supposedly revealed by Friesen's study of *abrichtung* in the German versions of Wittgenstein's *Investigations* and *Zettel*. The simplicity of Friesen's critique and his dismissiveness toward Wittgenstein scholars is astonishing. Guilt by association takes the place of sustained criticism of their well-received work. Based on a dictionary definition of *abrichtung*, and a few passages taken out of context or misinterpreted, he suggests (briefly, as though self-evident) that Smeyers and Burbules were wrong to build on Wittgenstein in advancing two-way communication between teacher-and-pupil and trainer-and-initiate. Winch was supposedly making a rather obvious mistake in using the concept of training in connection with human learning, as training supposedly pertains foremost to animals. Exonerating colleagues from Friesen's accusations of naiveté and poor translation (even moral taint), the defence wishes to theatrically parade before the jury the litany of reputable scholars across many fields constructively drawing on Wittgenstein. How did this academic community (beyond Huemer 2006) escape noticing the horror and darkness lurking in Wittgenstein's use of the word 'training'? Instead, the defence calls on Wittgenstein to testify.

Of the thousands of remarks that comprise Wittgenstein's later philosophy, Friesen is missing ones like these, which seek to describe (cf. PI §107) rather than prescribe how we learn concepts, and that point to the background context needed to absorb things like scientific concepts and procedures:

> One of the things we always do when discussing a word is ask how we were taught it. …Cf. How did we learn 'I dreamt so and so'? The interesting point is that we didn't learn it by

necessary in teaching and learning and induction into forms of life. It would also have to acknowledge the close connection of many influential Wittgenstinian terms and conceptions—from ostensive definition, rule-following and forms of life to language-games—with this apparently necessary, arbitrary brutality. Finally, it would have to reflect further on Wittgenstein's familiar claims; for example, that explanations come to an end somewhere" (1953, p. 5) in the light of Abrichtung. In many important cases, one could only conclude, explanation is forcefully brought to an end before it can even begin.

> being shown a dream. If you ask yourself how a child learns 'beautiful', 'fine', etc., you find he learns them roughly as interjections. (LC 1–2)
>
> Consider that you have to *teach* the child the *concept.* Thus you have to teach it evidence (the law of evidence, so to speak). …Remarkable the concept to which this game of evidence belongs. (LW I, p. 55e)

Overlooking such passages on learning, Friesen instead lifts from their context a few phrases that mention 'training': omitting the series of remarks where Wittgenstein builds a picture of how it is we come to hold some things *as* true or certain, and beyond doubt. For instance, Friesen latches onto Wittgenstein's remark that 'Any explanation has its foundation in training. (Educators ought to remember this.)' (Z§419). What is missing behind this dramatic pronouncement is the *stromatic* buildup or 'connective tissue', and moreover the philosophical significance of Wittgenstein's reflection on teaching a pupil who resists lessons that introduce our shared techniques and *bedrock* for acting in and investigating the world. It requires wider textual investigation to make reasonable connections and to judge these seemingly unrelated remarks:

> How does it come about that doubt is not subject to arbitrary choice? – And that being so – might not a child doubt everything because it was so remarkably talented? (Z §409)
>
> A person can doubt only if he has learned certain things…. (Z §410)
>
> Imagine that a child was quite specially clever, so clever that he could at once be taught the doubtfulness of the existence of all things. So he learns from the beginning: "That is probably a chair."
>
> And now how does he learn the question: "It is also really a chair?" –
>
> Am I doing child psychology? – I am making a connection between the concept of teaching and the concept of meaning. (Z §412)
>
> …There isn't any question of certainty or uncertainty yet in their language-game. Remember: they are learning to *do* something. (Z §416)
>
> To begin by teaching someone "That looks red" makes no sense. For he must say that spontaneously once he has learnt what "red" means, i.e., has learnt the technique of using the word. (Z §418)
>
> Any explanation has its foundation in training. (Educators ought to remember this.) (Z §419)

Fann (1971, 44) remarks on Z §412 (above) that 'Only an elementary-school teacher could have thought of making this connection'. For needed background beyond biography, these remarks can be paired with earlier ones in the same (posthumously edited) text, helping us understand Wittgenstein's purpose in the opening scenes and subsequent rule-following series of the *Investigations*—also showing how through alternate training we can generate a different perspective or 'way of life' (cf. PI §630).

> I cannot describe how (in general) to employ rules, except by *teaching* you, *training* you to employ rules. (Z§318)
>
> I want to say: an education quite different from ours might also be the foundation of quite different concepts. For here life would run on differently. (Z §387–88; cf. PI, p. 230)

The above references to ‘chairs’ being real are developed more fully in Z §413, where Wittgenstein considers whether it would actually make a difference if the parents of children were realists or idealists, if both sets had to teach their offspring to respond to simple instructions such as ‘take a seat’ or ‘bring me a chair’. Characteristically, he dissolves the metaphysical difference by focusing attention on their common training: ‘What will the children be taught?’ Certainly not to express doubt about the existence of the chair they take. After considering the similarity in training, he concludes by asking: ‘Then where will be the difference between what the idealist-educated children say and the realist ones?’ (Z §413).

The cases used in this *Zettel* series also relate to his parable of the intransigent pupil in *On Certainty*. Once perhaps a cause for great frustration in his own experience as an elementary teacher, it later has deeper significance in terms of epistemology: how we come to regard things (indubitably) *as true* despite a lack of sufficient evidence, reasons or the external verification logical positivism demands.

> A pupil and a teacher. The pupil will not let anything be explained to him, for he continually interrupts with doubts, for instance as to the existence of things, the meaning of words, etc. The teacher says ‘Stop interrupting me and do as I tell you. So far your doubts make no sense at all.’ (OC §310)
>
> Perhaps the teacher will get a bit impatient, but think that the boy will grow out of asking such questions. (OC §314)
>
> That is to say, the teacher will feel that this is not really a legitimate question at all. And it would be just the same if the pupil cast doubt on the uniformity of nature, that is to say on the justification of inductive arguments. – The teacher would feel that this was only holding them up, that this way the pupil would only get stuck and make no progress. – And he would be right. It would be as if someone were looking for some object in a room; he opens a drawer and doesn’t see it there; then he closes it again, waits, and opens it once more to see if perhaps it isn’t there now, and keeps on like that. He has not learned to look for things. And in the same way this pupil has not learned how to ask questions. He has not learned *the* game that we are trying to teach him. (OC §315)
>
> This doubt isn’t one of the doubts in our game. (But not as if we *chose* this game!) (OC §317)

What is at play here is not advice on pedagogy (harsh or otherwise), but one of the central problems haunting philosophy for millennia: whether our words must refer to objects (depict states-of-affairs, as Wittgenstein’s *Tratcatus* suggested, as the test for sensefulness), and our propositions or truth claims correspond to an external reality (which Rorty, who after Wittgenstein popularized the term ‘linguistic turn’, sought to smash in his groundbreaking work: *Philosophy in the Mirror of Nature*, 1979). Wittgenstein’s reason for entertaining these situations of children language learning belongs to his later project of repudiating the verificationist demands of logical positivism, where he too earlier pictured meaning as resting on correspondence with an external world. The ‘exercises’ he is running us through (see McClure 2017), as though we were now in his elementary classroom, are intended to dispel this faulty picture that holds us captive (PI §115).

> I used at one time to say that, in order to get clear how a sentence is used, it was a good idea to ask the question: "How would one try to verify such an assertion?" But that's just one way among others of getting clear about the use of a word or sentence. For example, another question which is often very useful to ask oneself is: "How is the word learned?" But some people have turned this suggestion about asking for the verification into a dogma – as if I'd been advancing a *theory* about meaning. (Gasking and Jackson 1967, 54)

It is this larger issue that is at stake when Wittgenstein pauses to reflect on how we learn to use colour words, in Z §418 above (see also Ch 3) or in PI §33 on the difficulty of pointing to the right colour blue, as of the sky.

> The agreement, the harmony, of thought and reality consists in this: if I say falsely that something is *red*, then, for all that, it isn't *red*. And when I want to explain the word "*red*" to someone, in the sentence 'That is not red,' I do it by pointing to something red. (OC §429)

> Teaching is central to this gradual process by which we adopt a shared worldview ('or better a worldpicture', *weltbild*, OC §§146–7, 262; see Ch 4), including such taken-for-granted concepts as colours and techniques such as mathematics (see PI, p. 225), or basic propositions (world-pictures) such as the sphericity of the earth (OC §§94, 219–220). Like ostensive definitions and the use of chess pieces, we absorb these from our background and our exposure to or training in many other games.

> The propositions describing this world-view might be part of a kind of mythology. And their role is like that of rules of a game; and the game can be learned purely practically, without learning any explicit rules." (OC §94; see §§95–97 above)

Wittgenstein's parable of the doubting pupil shows how our students come to believe and build upon what is found in textbooks (OC §§310–15). The training he depicts, in other words, has everything to do with how we come to believe things to be certain (see OC §336 in Ch 4) and react to signs or truth claims through our immersive enculturation into the language and practices that comprise our *second nature*.

> But doesn't anything physical correspond to it? I do not deny that. (And suppose it were merely our habituation to *these* concepts, to these language-games? But I am not saying that it is so.) If we teach a human being such-and-such a technique by means of examples – that he then proceeds like *this* and not *that* in a particular new case, or that in this case he gets stuck, and thus that this and not that is the 'natural' continuation for him: this of itself is an extremely important fact of nature. (Z §355)

> Well, if everything speaks for an hypothesis and nothing against it – is it then certainly true? One may designate it as such. – But does it certainly agree with reality, with the facts? With this question you are already going around in a circle.
>
> To be sure there is justification; but justification comes to an end. (OC §191–92)

Instead of seeking deeper forms of verification, Wittgenstein's post-foundationalism challenges us to accept impermanent and shifting ground for our certainties.

> I have arrived at the rock bottom of my convictions. …And one might almost say that these foundation walls are carried by the whole house. (OC §248)

> The difficulty is to realize the groundlessness of our believing. (OC §166)
>
> At the foundation of well-founded belief lies belief that is not founded. (OC §253)

Returning to our polemic, Friesen characterizes his method of interpretation as the 'German first approach', but we would describe it instead as a form of blatant decontextualization. Suggesting a gestalt switch, such as Wittgenstein illustrates in Part II of the *Investigations* (PI, p. 186) with Jastrow's duck–rabbit, Friesen replaces the English rabbit ('training') with a German Sheppard (*abrichtung*).

> To consider the possible implications of the term *Abrichtung* for Wittgenstein's late thought, I believe it is necessary to effect a change or shift in the perspective from which it is generally viewed and in the context in which his work is generally placed. To over-simplify, this is a shift from what might be called an 'English-language' to a 'German-language' perspective. It is a shift whose intrinsic complexity is compounded by the fact that Wittgenstein was active in both of these linguistic and cultural milieus, and that he is interpreted variously in each. (Friesen 2017, 73)

He systematically substitutes for English 'training' a harsh interpretation of *abrichung*, essentially reading into Wittgenstein a level of severity and passivity in the pupil that is simply not there in the remarks that comprise Wittgenstein's texts.[22] Going back to PI §5–6, the context for highlighting our rudimentary training into language was gradually acquiring the necessary background context for ostensive definitions of words.

> One can also imagine someone's having learnt the game [chess] without ever learning or formulating rules. He might have learnt quite simple board-games first, by watching, and have progressed to more and more complicated ones. (PI §31)

We cannot imagine explaining the use of pieces like 'the king' unless they have prior training:

> "This is the king" (or "This is called the 'king'") are a definition only if the learner already 'knows what a piece in a game is'. That is, if he has already played other games, or has watched other playing and 'understood' – *and similar things*. Further, only under these conditions will he be able to ask relevantly in the course of learning the game: "what do you call this?" – that is, this piece in a game. (PI §31)

It is laughable to suggest that there is any 'brutality' in these opening, emblematic scenes, or later in PI §§207–8 discussing how the pupil follows a numerical rule (e.g. of adding 2+100 but not being sure whether this rule holds at 1000), where the imaginary teacher uses words of encouragement and discouragement, exaggerated facial expressions, or guides the pupil's hand, etc. Ignoring these well-known cases, Friesen interjects the notion—foreign to Wittgenstein's lexicon—of breaking the pupil's 'will'. And here, especially, he has strayed from home, or 'gone on holiday' in reading Wittgenstein (see PI §38). Passages like this resonate like poorly played notes:

---

[22]As a thought-experiment, imagine someone discovers that the Greek word for 'virtue', *aretai*, is derived from Ares—the god of war, and thus that virtue was modelled in antiquity on a Spartan form as 'virulence' or athletic and martial prowess. One would not do well to substitute this meaning into Plato's Socratic dialogues or Aristotle's *Nicomachean Ethics*!

> Wittgenstein's portrayal of learners as passive and subservient, of training as drill, as a kind of breaking of the will, of orders, automatic and unthinking responses is rather unambiguous. (Friesen 2017, 71)

Unambiguous? we ask. Having substituted terms, Friesen now concludes that those English readers still using Wittgenstein are naïvely unfounded.

> In the light of these re-readings, interpretations of Wittgenstein's philosophy as one germane to progressive and contemporary educational thought and practices appear at least questionable if not untenable. (72)

Searching out instances where Wittgenstein refers to *abrichtung* and swapping terms (a kind of conjuring trick), Friesen is missing the wider context in which Wittgenstein's portrayal of 'training' occurs. Countering this misreading, David Bakhurst (2015, 306)[23] offers insight on interpreting Wittgenstein: here more broadly defending McDowell's explanation of training into second nature, and education as striving for autonomy within the 'space of reasons' (contra Rödl 2016).

> It has been noted that the term Wittgenstein uses, 'Abrichtung', is reserved for the training of animals and is not used of children. Critics are quick to seize on this and lament the 'brutal' character of Wittgenstein's view of teaching. We should not be too quick, however, to jump on the critics' bandwagon. 'Abrichtung' is not the only expression Wittgenstein uses that is translated as 'training'. There is also 'Unterricht' – meaning 'teaching', 'tuition' or 'instruction' – which has no such unfortunate connotations. Moreover, Wittgenstein sometimes uses 'abrichten' in tandem with terms for teaching such as 'lehren' or 'beibringen'.

In addition to his more expanded usage of interrelated educational terms, Wittgenstein was explicit about using scenes of training for heuristic purposes, to shed light on how we learn language and mathematics from infancy. Recall Wittgenstein's explanation of intent:

> It dispenses the fog to study the phenomena of language in primitive kinds of application in which one can command a clear view of the aim and functioning of words.

---

[23]Bakhurst (2015) was defending the very idea of initiation into humanity through acquisition of our second nature, as well as the educational goal of autonomy, from a critique delivered by Rödl (2016). (Both papers originate with papers delivered at a conference in 2013.) Rödl's argument against *abrichten* and second nature stems from his metaphysical argument, based on Aristotle's *De Anima,* that reason is already a part of human nature. Listening to Rödl deliver a brilliant but perplexing lecture on this topic (Queens University, Kingston, 2017), in which he further denied that teaching is not an art, brings to mind Wittgenstein's jest about the apparent silliness of metaphysical discourse:

> I am sitting with a philosopher in the garden; he says again and again 'I know that that's a tree', pointing to a tree that is near us. Someone else arrives and hears this, and I tell him: 'This fellow isn't insane. We are only doing philosophy. (OC §467)

Bakhurst (2017) also suggests following Williams' (1984/1999) account of this problem around training.

> A child uses such primitive forms of language when it learns to talk. Here the teaching of language is not explanation, but training. (PI §5)

An example of Friesen's misinterpretation through decontextualization can be found in the following case he elaborates, where he chastises Wittgenstein for discarding a broader range in usage of the word 'understanding'—something that, if it were true, would go against Wittgenstein's insistence in the *Investigations* that we look carefully at the myriad uses of words in various language-games (PI §23; see Ch 1). Friesen again projects the language of behaviourism in writing the following (2017, 69–70):

> There are for example passages from his *Lectures* (1932–1935) in which Wittgenstein again insists that training is comparable to 'drill,' and that language learning is indeed analogous to the most arbitrary exercises in stimulus and response:
>
> Training can be described as consisting of two steps (1) the trainer's doing certain things, (2) the occurrence of certain reactions on the part of the subject, with the possibility of improvement. Teaching a language *always* depends on a training which presupposes that the subject reacts. If the subject does not react in a given case, that is, does not understand. Reference to understanding will then not appear in the description of the training. But nothing is omitted from the description by omitting reference to understanding. (p. 102)
>
> Wittgenstein is not only describing training in the austere terms of the subject's reaction to a trainer 'doing certain things,' he is further arguing that any reference to 'understanding' in such an account at most refers to the presence or absence of an appropriate 'reaction.' Any additional connotations or denotations carried by the word 'understanding,' Wittgenstein believes, can simply be discarded.

Wittgenstein was adamant that philosophers not interfere in or fix the ways in which language is actually employed (PI §130–33): instead of discarding words, they are to 'leave everything as it is' (PI §§124 and 126) and merely describe usage (PI §107–09). What Wittgenstein means by identifying 'understanding' as 'correct reaction to the training' is simply the observation that correct reaction is our only criterion for identifying the achievement of understanding. Why? We have no access to the inner thoughts of the person who supposedly understands.

> The origin and the primitive form of the language game is a reaction; only from this can more complicated forms develop.
>
> Language – I want to say – is a refinement, 'in the beginning was the deed.' (CV 31e; see Ch 3)

Instead of reducing our concept of 'understanding' as Friesen claims, Wittgenstein opens it through investigation of the role it plays in our *language-games* or everyday practices, into which we have been trained. Why, he asks, do we sometimes feel that a word or phrase could not be replaced with another, but other times alternatives are found?

> There might also be a language in whose use the 'soul' of the words played no part. In which, for example, we had no objection to replacing one word by another arbitrary one of our own invention.[24] (PI §530)
>
> We speak of understanding a sentence in the sense in which it can be replaced by another which says the same; but also in the sense in which it cannot be replaced by any other. (Any more than one musical theme can be replaced by another.)
>
> In the one case the thought in the sentence is something common to different sentences; in the other, something that is expressed only by these words in these positions. (Understanding a poem.) (PI §531)
>
> Then has 'understanding' two different meanings here? – I would rather say that these kinds of use of 'understanding' make up its meaning, make up my *concept* of understanding.
>
> For I *want* to apply the word 'understanding' to all this. (PI §532)

Concluding our cross-examination of Friesen: After a more interesting segment on Freud that nevertheless hazards into psychological profiles and over generalization,[25] in closing Friesen (2017, 76) exhibits a strange form of triumphalism (self-overcoming the negativity of *abrichtung*) in twisting Wittgenstein into a dark and tragic figure. Anyone who has read Wittgenstein's biographies realizes quickly that Wittgenstein is a tragic and hermetic figure, prone to suicide and isolation, but that he struggled to improve his character and endure. On his deathbed he declared: 'Tell them I have had a wonderful life' (Malcolm 1966, 100). Labelling him a 'tragic philosopher of education' adds nothing to the conversation, and suggesting that his use in education is also somehow misguided grossly distorts the picture of how he has been taken up in the field.

> In the end, Wittgenstein's view of education culminates in a tragic paradox. This is one that most scholars in education and perhaps even philosophy would be tempted to avoid or at least minimize: that what makes us human, what brings us into any and all forms of human life is precisely the inhumanity of our conditioning and adaptation to them. Openly acknowledging this inhumanity does not come easily. However, it can lead to very different understandings of education from one jejunely progressivist or reductively cognitivist and biologistic.

Wittgenstein did indeed refer, in the Preface to the *Investigations* (PI, p. viii), to the post-war (1945) era as a 'dark age' but that was motivated largely by resignations of a 'genius' figure in the face of feeling he could not convey his thoughts to even well-educated people.

> It is not impossible that it should fall to the lot of this work, in its poverty and in the darkness of this time, to bring light into one brain or another – but, of course, it is not likely. (PI, p. viii)

---

[24]It is a great temptation to try to make the spirit explicit. (CV 8e)

[25]In self-affirming his *abrichung* reading, and now reaching out to the culture in which Wittgenstein wrote (supposedly after Janik and Toulmin (1973) but seemingly unaware of Burbules' work on this earlier; see Ch 9 in Peters and Marshall 1999), Friesen writes (75): 'Freud and Wittgenstein, of course, view these processes of "humanization" as necessarily entailing renunciation and brutality.'

> I never more than half succeed in expressing what I want to express. Actually not as much as that, but no more than a tenth. That is still worth something. Often my writing is nothing but 'stuttering'. (CV 18e)

As Savivkey (2017, 77; cf. 1999) also notes, Wittgenstein's view of working through his material on one's own fits with the Austrian education reforms into which he was trained and practiced as a teacher. In one of Wittgenstein's rare statements about pedagogy, promoting the use of his *Dictionary for Elementary Schools* over peer-correction, he is certainly *not* talking about drilling or debasing pupils but allowing them to master the language (see PI §538) by taking responsibility for their own learning (what Medina 2002, 2004 calls normative training towards autonomy within the rules; see Ch 3):

> Only a dictionary makes it possible to hold the student completely responsible for the spelling of what he has written because it furnishes him with reliable measures for finding and correcting his mistakes, provided he has a mind to do so. It is, however, absolutely necessary that the student corrects his composition on his own. He should feel that he is the author of his work and he alone should be responsible for it. It is also this independent correction that enables the teacher to get a correct picture of the student's knowledge and mental capacities. The exchange of exercise-books and the reciprocal correction of compositions results in a blurred image, so to speak, of the abilities of the class. (PO 15)

Instead of being a pedagogue restricted to regimes of training and the breaking of the will, his approach to teaching and his style of philosophical writing—what McClure (2017) likens to exercises in a workbook—exemplifies the central tenet of the reform movement: learn-by-doing or *Arbietschule* (learning-by-doing) over *abrichtung*.

> I should not like my writing to spare other people the trouble of thinking. But, if possible, to stimulate someone to thoughts of his own. (PI, p. x).

Wittgenstein had little interest in founding a school to carry out his work; instead, he preferred that there be a change in the way people think and act (CV 61).

> [I believe it might interest a philosopher, one who can think himself, to read my notes. For even if I have hit the mark only rarely, he would recognize what targets I had been ceaselessly aiming at.] (OC §387)

### 2.3.3 *Aesthetic Judgment*

> My style is like bad musical composition. (CV 39e)

Another example may help here, dispelling notions of brutal training[26] if we picture instead the rigorous process of exercise and discipline needed in becoming an accomplished pianist. How do music instructors know for instance when a student has mastered a piece of piano music, or now plays the score with artistry: 'depth of feeling' instead of mechanically? (Again, compare reading like an automaton, in PI §157.)[27] These questions of aesthetic judgement occupied Wittgenstein's thought because he grew up in a musically inclined (see Chap. 1) family, [28] While teaching in rural Austria, he joined company with two other colleagues who could play music in his room, carrying on a tradition that was rather foreign to the rustic place in which he came to reside. In terms of his own clarinet playing, Wittgenstein was self-taught,[29] and so imposing a regime of training on himself in order to achieve an acceptable standard. 'In what we call the Arts', he notes, 'a person who has judgment develops', [sic] allowing us 'to distinguish between a person who knows what he is talking about and a person who doesn't' (CV §17, 6e). Wittgenstein's point, both with reference to the passage cited by Friesen (LC 102) and in the series of reflections below, is that in applauding a fantastic pianist we do not have to add to this cultured reaction words like 'she really understands Chopin'. How do you know someone 'understands it' (Z §159)?

> Appreciating music is a manifestation of the life of mankind. How should we describe it to someone? Well, I suppose we should first have to describe music. The we would have to describe how human beings react to it. But is that all we need to do, or must we also teach him to understand it for himself? Well, getting him to understand and giving him an explanation that does not achieve this will be "teaching him what understanding is" in *different* senses of that phrase. And again, teaching him to understand poetry or painting may contribute to teaching him what is involved in understanding music. (CV 70e)

> If a theme, a phrase, suddenly means something to you, you don't have to be able to explain it… Do not forget that a poem, even though it is composed in the language of information, is not used in the language-game of giving information. (Z §158)

---

[26]In Z §383, he imagines a tribe where such severe training has occurred, that people do not respond to pain as we do: never speaking of feelings of pain or using interjections to express hurt. Not sharing in their extreme regime of training, we cannot find our feet with such people. (Z §390)

[27]Sometimes a sentence can be understood only if it is read at the right tempo. My sentences are all supposed to be read slowly. (CV 57e)

I really want my copious punctuation marks to slow down the speed of reading. Because I should like to be read slowly. (As I myself read.) (CV 68e)

[28]Ravel's 'Concerto for one hand', as Paul lost an arm in World War I.

[29]McGuiness (1988, 32) notes, alluding to religion and the humanities: 'It seems that Ludwig preferred subjects that he could teach himself, as he later taught himself the clarinet….'

> Feelings, therefore, belong to the mystical realm that cannot be put into words. Feelings express themselves in art most effectively when they are not discussed. (Z §160)
>
> For how can it be explained what 'expressive playing' is? Certainly not by anything that accompanies the playing. – What is needed for the explanation? One might say: a culture. – If someone is brought up in a particular culture – and then reacts to music in such-and-such a way, you can teach him the use of the phrase "expressive playing". (Z§164)

Almost ineluctable, but nevertheless we might discuss feelings of understanding art, on occasion, as in taking up a conversation about a recital or painting we saw recently. 'It is possible … to say a *great deal* about a fine aesthetic difference,' Wittgenstein notes. What matters most, though, is that in gradually finding *apt* expressions we explore the *extensive ramifications*, connotative range or *field of force* of our words (PI II, p. 219; cf. PI §117).

> It is not only difficult to describe what appreciation consists in, but impossible. To describe what it consists in we would have to describe the whole environment. (CV 7e)
>
> The words we call expressions of aesthetic judgment play a very complicated role, but a very definite role, in what we call a culture of a period. To describe their use or to describe what you mean by a cultured taste, you have to describe a culture. (CV 8e)
>
> We think we have to talk about aesthetic judgments like 'This is beautiful', but we find that if we have to talk about aesthetic judgments we don't find these words at all, but a word used something like a gesture, accompanying a complicated activity. (CV 11e)[30]
>
> In art it is hard to say anything as good: as saying nothing. (CV 23e)
>
> Piano playing, a dance of human fingers. (CV 36e)
>
> Understanding and explaining a musical phrase. – Sometimes the simplest explanation is a gesture; on another occasion it might be a dance step, or words describing a dance. … (CV 69e)

Wittgenstein's depiction of how pupils demonstrate understanding in mathematics and music points to the normative learning process (PI §§150–51; see Ch 3): Without recourse to explicit criteria or rules somehow outside the practices, the expert observer immanently discerns correct performance, where evident 'mastery of techniques' is our criterion of success.

> – To obey a rule, to make report, to give an order, to play a game of chess, are *customs* (uses, institutions).
>
> To understand a sentence means to understand a language. To understand a language means to be master of a technique. (PI §199 cf. PI, p. 228)

Agreement of the masters becomes the standard, as those operating autonomously within the rules are in a position to distinguish between 'a normal and abnormal learner's reactions' to instruction (PI §143).

---

[30]Don't imagine a description which you have never heard, which describes an attitude in unheard of detail. …An attitude is pretty well described by the position of the body. This is a good description. But accurate? (CV 35e).

> And here the strange thing is that when I am quite certain of how the words are used, have no doubt about it, I can still give no *grounds* for my way of going on… (OC §307)
>
> If someone asked us "but is that true?" we might say "yes" to him; and if he demanded grounds we might say "I can't give you any grounds, but if you learn more you too will think the same".
>
> If this didn't come about, that would mean that he couldn't for example learn history. (OC §206)

Every attempt at specifying the circumstances giving meaning to either aesthetic or teaching acts depends upon further background for its coherence. Consider how teachers know when pupils correctly use the word 'think'. Wittgenstein reminds us that we know correct applications, or recognize them, even though we cannot describe the complex circumstances that underlie normal usage.

> One learns the word 'think', i.e. its use, under certain circumstances, which, however, one does not learn to describe. (Z §114)
>
> But I *can teach* a person the use of the word! For a description of the circumstances is not needed for that. (Z §115; cf. OC §545–8)

## References


Bakhurst, D. (2015). Training, transformation and education. *Royal Institute of Philosophy Supplement, 76,* 301–327.

Bakhurst, D. (2017). Wittgenstein and education (Foreword). In M. A. Peters & J. Stickney (Eds.), *A companion to Wittgenstein on education: Pedagogical investigations* (pp. v–xiii). Singapore: Springer.

Bartley, W., III. (1973). *Wittgenstein*. London: Quartet Books.

Burbules, N. (2017). Wittgenstein's metaphors and his pedagogical philosophy. In M. A. Peters & J. Stickney (Eds.), *A companion to Wittgenstein on education: Pedagogical investigations* (pp. 123–133). Singapore: Springer.

Burwood, S. (2017). "A spontaneous following": Wittgenstein, education and the limits of trust. In M. A. Peters & J. Stickney (Eds.), *A companion to Wittgenstein on education: Pedagogical investigations* (pp. 161–177). Singapore: Springer.

Cavell. J. (1979). *The claim of reason. Wittgenstein, skepticism, morality and tragedy.* Oxford and New York: Oxford University Press.

Cavell, J. (2005). *Philosophy the day after tomorrow*. Cambridge, MA: Harvard University Press.

Curry, M. (1989). Forms of life and geographical method. *Geographical Review, 79,* 280–296.

Curry, M. (2000). Wittgenstein and the fabric of everyday life. In M. Crang & N. Thrift (Eds.), *Thinking space*. London and New York: Routledge.

Elden, S. (2011). *Reintroducing Kant's geography*. Albany: State University of New York Press.

Emerson, R. W. (1965). The over-soul. In W. H. Gilman (Ed.), *Selected writings of Ralph Waldo Emerson*. New York: Signet Classic.

Fann, T. K. (1971). *Wittgenstein's conception of philosophy*. Berkeley: University of California Press.

Friesen, N. (2016). Lost in translation: Ludwig Wittgenstein, education and the question of abrichtung. (Presented at the Philosophy of Education Society annual meeting, Toronto, 2016); also found at http://blogs.ubc.ca/nfriesen/files/2015/08/wittgenstein-training.pdf.

Friesen, N. (2017). Training and *abrichtung*: Wittgenstein as a tragic philosopher of education. *Educational Philosophy and Theory, 49*(1), 68–77.

Gadamer, H.-J. (1977). *Philosophical hermeneutics* (D. E. Linge, Trans. & Ed.). Berkeley, Los Angeles, London: University of California Press.

Gasking, D. A. T., & Jackson, A. C. (1967). Wittgenstein as a teacher. In K. T. Fann (Ed.), *Ludwig Wittgenstein: The man and his philosophy* (pp. 49–55). Atlantic Highlands, NJ: Humanities Press.

Gasparatou, R. (2017). On "the temptation to attack common sense". In M. A. Peters & J. Stickney (Eds.), *A companion to Wittgenstein on education*: Pedagogical investigations, 275–286. Singapore: Springer.

Glock, H.-J. (1996). A Wittgenstein dictionary. Oxford: Blackwell.

Heidegger, M. (1977a). Building/dwelling/thinking. In D. Krell (Ed.), *Basic writings*. New York: Harper & Row.

Heidegger, M. (1977b). Poetically man dwells. In *Poetry, language, thought* (A. Hofstader, Trans.). New York: Harper Collins.

Heidegger, M., & Fink, E. (1970). *Heraclitus seminar*. Evanston, IL: Northwestern University Press.

Huemer, W. (2006). The transition from causes to norms: Wittgenstein on training. *Grazer Philosophiche Studien, 71,* 205–225.

Janik, A., & Toulmin, S. (1973). *Wittgenstein's Vienna*. New York: Simon and Schuster.

Jarman, D. (Director) (1993). *Wittgenstein*. Screenplay by D. Jarman, T. Eagleton, & K. Butler. UK: BFI Productions.

Kant, I. (1904). The educational theory of Immanuel Kant. Trans. and ed. with an introd. by E. Franklin Buchner. Philadelphia: Lippincott.

Kaufmann, W. (1966). *Hegel: A reinterpretation*. Garden City, NY: Doubleday Anchor.

Kern, A. (2017). *Sources of knowledge. On the concept of a rational capacity for knowledge* (D. Smyth, Trans.). Cambridge, MA: Harvard University Press.

Luntley, M. (2007). Learning, empowerment and judgement. *Educational Philosophy and Theory, 39*(4), 418–431.

Luntley, M. (2008). Training and learning [Response to Jeff Stickney]. *Educational Philosophy and Theory, 40*(5), 695–711.

Luntley, M. (2012). Training, training, training: The making of second nature and the roots of Wittgenstein's pragmatism. *European Journal of Pragmatism and American Philosophy. Symposia: Wittgenstein and Pragmatism a Reassessment, IV*(2), 88–104.

Luntley, M. (2017). Wittgenstein and the path of learning. In M. A. Peters & J. Stickney (Eds.), *A companion to Wittgenstein on education: Pedagogical investigations* (pp. 437–452). Singapore: Springer.

Macmillan, C. J. B. (1995). How not to learn: Reflections on Wittgenstein and learning. In J. Marshall & P. Smeyers (Eds.), *Philosophy and education: Accepting Wittgenstein's challenge*. Dordrecht, Boston and London: Kluwer Academic Publishers.

Malcolm, N. (1966). Ludwig Wittgenstein: A memoir. Oxford: Oxford University Press.

Marshall, J. D. (1995). Wittgenstein and Foucault: Resolving Philosophical Puzzles. In J. Marshall & P. Smeyers (eds), Philosophy and Education: Accepting Wittgenstein's Challenge, 205–220. Dordrecht, Boston & London: Kluwer Academic Publishers. Reprinted from Studies in Philosophy and Education, 14, nos. 2–3 (1995).

Marshall, J., & Smeyers, P. (Eds.). (1995). *Philosophy and education: Accepting Wittgenstein's challenge*. Dordrecht, Boston and London: Kluwer Academic Publishers.

May, J. A. (1970), *Kant's concept of geography and its relation to recent geographical thought* (xi, 280 p). Published for the University of Toronto Department of Geography by University of Toronto Press

McClure, E. (2017). Do your exercises: Reader participation in Wittgenstein's investigations. In M. A. Peters & J. Stickney (Eds.), *A companion to Wittgenstein on education: Pedagogical investigations* (pp. 147–159). Singapore: Springer.

McGuiness, B. (1988). Young Ludwig, 1889–1921. In *Wittgenstein: A life*. Los Angeles, Berkeley, London: University of California Press.
Medina, J. (2002). *The unity of Wittgenstein's philosophy. Necessity, intelligibility, and normativity*. Albany: State University of New York Press.
Medina, J. (2004). Wittgenstein's social naturalism: The idea of '*second nature*'. In D. Moyal-Sharrock (Ed.), *The third Wittgenstein: The post-investigation works*. Aldershot: Ashgate.
Monk, R. (1991). *Wittgenstein: The duty of genius*. London: Penguin Books.
Monk, R. (2001). Philosophical biography: The very idea. In J. C. Klagge (Ed.), *Wittgenstein. Biography and philosophy* (pp. 3–16). Cambridge: Cambridge University Press.
Nietzsche, F. (1965). *Schopenhauer as educator* (J. W. Hillesheim & M. R. Simpson, Trans.). Chicago: Henry Regnery.
Peters, M. A. (1995). Philosophy and education: 'After' Wittgenstein. In J. Marshall & P. Smeyers (Eds.),*Philosophy and education: Accepting Wittgenstein's challenge* (pp.189–204). Dordrecht, Boston and London: Kluwer Academic Publishers.
Peters, M. A. (2017). Wittgenstein's trials, teaching and Cavell's romantic "figure of the child". In M. A. Peters & J. Stickney (Eds.), *A companion to Wittgenstein on education: Pedagogical investigations* (pp. 101–113). Singapore: Springer.
Peters, M. A., & Marshall, J. (1999). *Wittgenstein: Philosophy, postmodernism, pedagogy*. Westport, CT and London: Bergin and Garvey.
Peters, M. A., Burbules, N., & Smeyers, P. (2008). *Showing and doing: Wittgenstein as a pedagogical philosopher*. London: Routledge.
Peters, M. A., & Stickney, J. (Eds.). (2017). *A companion to Wittgenstein on education: Pedagogical investigations* (pp. 101–113). Singapore: Springer.
Rödl, S. (2016). Education and autonomy. *Journal of Philosophy of Education, 50*(1).
Rorty, R. (1979). *Philosophy and the mirror of nature*. Princeton, NJ: Princeton University Press.
Ryle, G. (1949). *The concept of mind*. London: Hutchinson.
Savickey, B. (1999). *Wittgenstein's art of investigation*. London, New York: Routledge.
Savickey, B. (2017). Wittgenstein's philosophy: *Viva voce*. In M. A. Peters & J. Stickney (Eds.), *A companion to Wittgenstein on education: Pedagogical investigations* (pp. 63–78). Singapore: Springer.
Smeyers, P., & Burbules, N. C. (2005/2006/2010). Practice: A central educational concept. In K. Howe (Ed.), *Philosophy of Education Society yearbook, 2005* (pp. 336–334). San Francisco: Paper given at the annual meeting of PES.
Smeyers, P., & Burbules, N. C. (2006). Education as initiation into practices. *Educational Theory, 56*(4), 439–449.
Smeyers, P., & Burbules, N. (2010). Education as initiation into practices. In M. A. Peters, N. C. Burbules, & P. Smeyers (Eds.), *Showing and doing: Wittgenstein as a pedagogical philosopher* (pp. 183–198). New York, NY: Routledge.
Standish, P., Smeyers, P., & Smith, R. (Eds.). (2007). *The therapy of education. Philosophy, happiness and personal growth*. Basingstoke: Palgrave Macmillan.
Stickney, J. (2005). Teaching and learning in Wittgenstein's philosophic method. In K. Howe (Ed.), *Philosophy of Education Society yearbook, 2005* (pp. 299–308). Paper given at the PES annual meeting, San Francisco.
Stickney, J. (2008). Training and mastery of techniques in Wittgenstein's later philosophy: A response to Michael Luntley. *Educational Philosophy and Theory, 40*(5), 678–694.
von Goethe, J. W. (2001). *Wilhelm Meister's apprenticeship. The Harvard classics shelf of fiction* (Vol. XIV). UK: Bartleby.
Winch, C. (2002). *The philosophy of human learning*. London: Routledge.
Winch, C. (2018). Wittgenstein on training. Comment on Norm Friesen. *Educational Philosophy and Theory* (forthcoming, under review).
Williams, M. (1984). The significance of learning in Wittgenstein's later philosophy. *Canadian Journal of Philosophy, 24*(2), 173–203. (Reprinted as *The philosophical significance of*

*learning in the later Wittgenstein, in her Wittgenstein, mind and meaning: Towards a social conception of mind*, 1999, London: Routledge.)

Williams, M. (1999). The etiology of the obvious. Wittgenstein and the elimination of indeterminacy. In Wittgenstein, mind and meaning. Toward a social conception of mind (Ch 8). London & New York: Routledge.

Williams, M. (2010). *Blind obedience*. London: Routledge.

Wittgenstein, L. (1953). *Philosophical investigations*. Oxford: Blackwell (PI).

Wittgenstein, L. (1956). *Remarks on the foundation of mathematics* (G. E. M. Anscombe, Trans.). Oxford: Basil Blackwell (RFM).

Wittgenstein, L. (1967a). *Zettel* (G. E. M. Anscombe, Trans.). Oxford: Basil Blackwell (Z).

Wittgenstein, L. (1967b). In C. Barrett (Ed.), *Lectures and conversations on aesthetics, psychology and religious belief*. Berkeley: University of California Press (LC).

Wittgenstein, L. (1968). *Philosophical investigations* (3rd ed., G. E. M. Anscombe, Trans.). Oxford: Basil Blackwell (PI§, or PI, pg.)

Wittgenstein, L. (1969a). *The blue and brown books: Preliminary studies for the 'Philosophical Investigations'*. Oxford: Basil Blackwell (BB).

Wittgenstein, L. (1969b). *On certainty* (D. Paul & G. E. M. Anscombe, Trans.). Oxford: Basil Blackwell (OC).

Wittgenstein, L. (1976). In C. Diamond (Ed.), *Wittgenstein's lectures on the foundations of mathematics*. New York: Harvester Press (LFM).

Wittgenstein, L. (1980). In G. H. von Wright (Ed.) in collaboration with H. Nyman. *Culture and value* (P. Winch, Trans.). Oxford: Basil Blackwell (CV).

Wittgenstein, L. (1980). In G. E. M. Anscombe & G. H. von Wright (Eds.), *Remarks on the philosophy of psychology* (Vol. 2, G. E. M. Anscombe, Trans.). Oxford: Basil Blackwell (RPP).

Wittgenstein, L. (1993). Preface to the 'dictionary for elementary schools'. In J. C. Klagge & A. Nordmann (Eds.), *Philosophical occasions (1912–1951)*. Indianapolis and Cambridge: Hackett (PO).

# Chapter 3
# Wittgenstein as a School Teacher

## 3.1 Introduction[1]

Not seeking to extract pedagogical theory from Wittgenstein's philosophy, here we survey some of the background on Wittgenstein's teaching in so far as it may be relevant to his later philosophy and to discussion of issues related to teaching, learning, and philosophy of education. Acknowledging the boundaries Wittgenstein drew between empirical and philosophical questions, here we set Wittgenstein's later remarks on training against the background of his own elementary school teaching in rural Austria (1920–26), sorting empirical matters related to education from his philosophical concern with the acquisition and judgment of meaning. Interested in securing learning in his elementary classroom, he later came to distinguish such causal inquiries from philosophical inspection of grammatical problems (PI §122).[2] In this move, training is the avenue leading us into felicitous performance of language-games (including math and music notation), but meaning (an ontological concern with significance) is socially governed in terms of our usage and judgment, and is neither reducible to its prerequisite nor closed from change.

Hunter (1985, see Ch 4) illustrates this beautifully through the case of a frustrated mathematics teacher struggling with the problem of 'retelling' (not merely repeating) instructions in such a way as to clarify intended rules for the perplexed student. How does the teacher know when the pupil 'gets it'? Adeptly employing words or rules within their appropriate connotative, axiomatic and grammatical

---

[1]Excerpt from Stickney (2017).

[2]Following convention, titles for Wittgenstein's works are abbreviated (PI = Philosophical Investigations, RFM = Remarks on the Foundation of Mathematics, OC = On Certainty, WL = Wittgenstein's Lectures, CV = Culture Value, PO = Philosophical Occasions), with section (§) or page number (p.), with full citation and initials (e.g. RFM) in the References. See Abbreviation list, p.ii??



M. A. Peters and J. Stickney, *Wittgenstein's Education: 'A Picture Held Us Captive'*, SpringerBriefs on Key Thinkers in Education
https://doi.org/10.1007/978-981-10-8411-9_3

ranges of usage, the pupil demonstrates learning achievement as a criterion for successful initiation into conventional practice or mastery of techniques (PI §199). Attention to training as the basis for judgment (PI, p. 227) sidesteps the vicious circularity, leaving shared practice as our 'ground' in an otherwise post-foundational epistemology.

## 3.2 Elementary School Teaching

> While at school our children get taught that water *consists* of the gases hydrogen and oxygen, or sugar of carbon, hydrogen and oxygen. Anyone who doesn't understand is stupid. The most important questions are concealed. (CV 71e)

When Wittgenstein moved to rural Austria to teach elementary school (1920–26), his sister (Hermine) protested that this 'was like using a precision instrument to open crates,' to which he replied that it was a better alternative to suicide—the unfortunate demise of two and possibly three of his older brothers (Bartley 1985, 37). Perhaps taken on as an escape from the world, like his subsequent gardening work in a monastery, he nevertheless embraced the challenge to become an educator and even wrote with enthusiasm to Russell about being 'happy in my work at school' (Monk 1990, 193). The difficult task often proved to be frustrating, however, partly because the cultivated aristocrat was out of place among rural, poor folk who found him 'strange' (Monk 1990, 194, 197). His teaching career ended after 6 years with an inquest into his well-documented use of corporal punishment (see Monk 1990, 194–5, e.g. accounts of pulling girls' hair and cuffing boys' ears, etc.). Wittgenstein's rather Nietzschean views of education appear untimely now.

> I think the way people are educated nowadays tends to diminish their capacity for suffering. At present a school is reckoned good 'if the children have a good time'. And that used not to be the criterion. Parents moreover want their children to grow up like themselves (only more so), but nevertheless subject them to an education quite different from their own. – Endurance of suffering isn't rated highly because there is supposed not to be any suffering – really it's out of date. (CV 71e)

Despite strict discipline, students later described Wittgenstein as a highly devoted if demanding teacher (see Bartley 1985; Monk 1990). In his elementary classroom, Wittgenstein assiduously compiled words students used, forming a reference dictionary. Edmonds and Eidnow (2001, 61) note that 'his dictionary was in keeping with the [reform] movement and the position in the *Investigations* that rural dialects could be in perfect order as they are.' Phillips (1977, 8, citing Bartley 1985, 117) claims that by keeping their own dictionary, Wittgenstein's students gained an appreciation of 'the ambiguity of their own usage of the language.' In this sense, Wittgenstein was conservator of the child's quotidian language: pedagogy congruent with his later philosophy—meaning-as-use (OC §61).

Wittgenstein's practical approach to teaching was somewhat in keeping with child-centred movements in Austria, in vogue while attending Vienna's Teacher Training College (1919–20; Phillips 1977, 7–10; Bartley 1974; see Savickey 1999, 2017).

> Consistent with Austrian school reform, Wittgenstein describes himself as a philosophical guide (LFM 44). And there is no better description of his method than 'learning by doing.' As late as 1948, he echoes Burger's 'work philosophy' when he writes: 'Anything your reader can do, leave to him' (CV 77e). In the preface to the *Investigations*, he also states: 'I should not like my writing to spare other people the trouble of thinking. But, if possible, to stimulate someone to thoughts of his own' (PI xe). The principles of self-activity and integrated instruction are exemplified in the participatory nature of Wittgenstein's classes and texts. Students and readers alike are called upon to reason and puzzle things out for themselves. '[Wittgenstein] remarked to the effect that it did not matter whether his results were true or not; what mattered was that "a method had been found"' (Fann 1969: 109–110; in Savickey 2017, 76–77)

Bartley, however, recalls Wittgenstein joking about these reforms: perhaps embracing the anti-scholastic spirit and practices, but amused by campaign rhetoric. Edmonds and Eidnow (2001, 61) also recall that 'Wittgenstein poked fun at the programme's 'more vulgar slogans and projects.' Wittgenstein was cautious about 'language gone on holiday' (PI §38): '...Don't let yourself be seduced by the terminology in common currency' (CV 74e). Citing Engelmann's (1967, 114–6) view that Wittgenstein learned from teaching young children how to better translate his own ideas, enabling him in the *Investigations* to convey his rather cryptic thoughts in the *Tractatus,* Eugene Hargrove embraces a sceptical reading of the Austrian school reform movement. Hargrove (1980, 461) captures the relevance of his teacher training by suggesting:

> we can see influence of Wittgenstein's time as a teacher on almost every page of the *Investigations*, .... Throughout his later philosophy, Wittgenstein often supported the points he was making by citing personal observations about children. It is these observations, which he made as school teacher and used as a pool of data later, that, as I see it, are the true influence on Wittgenstein's work, and not principles taught at the teachers college or waived in his face by school reformers.

That early teaching experience influenced Wittgenstein's later thinking at Cambridge is apparent from Wittgenstein's use of orthography as a paradigmatic case.

> One might think: if philosophy speaks of the use of the word "philosophy" there must be a second-order philosophy. But it is not so; it is, rather, like the case of orthography, which deals with the word "orthography" among others without being second-order. (PI §121)

Remarks on orthography adduce Wittgenstein's general attitude towards foundations, and our later flexibility within rules and practices—some of which may be arbitrary and open to revision.

> Just as in writing we learn a particular basic form of letters and then vary it later, so we learn first the stability of things as the norm, which is then subject to alteration. (OC §473)

Appealing to his superintendent's attention, Wittgenstein says his *Dictionary for Elementary Schools* (1926) has the goal 'to fill an urgent need with respect to the present teaching of orthography' (PO 15). Prefacing the dictionary 'to make intelligible his general plan', he justifies violating standard rules of alphabetical order, recognized for efficiency and logic. As though making a philosophical refutation, he argues it reduces slippage in learning:

> But if the purely alphabetic order inserts a heterogeneous word between two closely related ones, then in my opinion the alphabetic order demands too much from a child's power of abstraction. Thus, because of the comprehension of words and the highly important saving of space, the purely alphabetic order often cannot be recommended. Equally, each instance of clinging to a dogmatic principle leads to an arrangement that does not suit our purpose and has to be abandoned – even if this would make the author's work much easier. Rather, it is necessary to compromise again and again. (PO 23)

Acknowledging age-appropriate ranges for more demanding, abstract concepts, Wittgenstein's pedagogy sought to reduce what we may see through *On Certainty* as failure to concretize, or erosion of, *bedrock* (OC §94–98). Breaking convention, simplifying better secures learning, showing that teaching technique is not arbitrary. In courses requiring sequential learning, like math and language, it matters greatly whether and when certain content or skills are covered: indeed, mastered through a variety of means reaching students with diverse needs. As a practical art, teaching is closer to cooking in this regard, requiring savoir faire that teachers would find hard to articulate or pass onto novices undergoing teacher training (see PI, p. 227 on demonstrating or giving tips at best).

> Why don't I call cookery rules arbitrary, and why am I tempted to call the rules of grammar arbitrary? Because 'cookery' is defined by its end, whereas 'speaking' is not.... You cook badly if you are guided in your cooking by rules other than the right ones; but if you follow other rules than those of chess you are playing another game; and if you follow grammatical rules other than such-and-such ones, that does not mean you say something wrong, no, you are speaking of something else. (Z §320; cf. PI §§496–499)

Not just any game of learning-enhancement or engagement will do, but too often Ministries of Education (whether in 1920s Austria or those today) attend to creating new menus instead of actually improving the cooking.[3] Wittgenstein wanted to address this problem, first in his own classroom, and then widely in distributing his *Dictionary for Elementary Schools*. From what he refers to as his 'subjective view' it was pedagogically better to group families of words sharing etymological roots, even if this method 'clashes with the generally held principle of alphabetic order' (PO 21). Under alphabetic order, the words alt and Alter are broken up by a heterogeneous word, Altar:

| | |
|---|---|
| alt, das Alter | old, old age |
| der Altar | altar |
| D[d]as Alterum, altermümlich | antiquity, antique |

[3]Karl Popper did his doctorate in educational psychology in Vienna at the same time, and concluded that most education reforms were ideological rather than scientific (a case of employing his famous demarcation principle, showing teaching to be something not easily tested). (See Fuller 2004.)

As a 'good' teacher,[4] Wittgenstein was concerned with discovering effective techniques to enhance student learning, and he reflected on his own success. Pondering students' learning-slippage, he later remarked (1940):

> A teacher may get good, even astounding, results from his pupils while he is teaching them and yet not be a good teacher; because it may be that, while his pupils are directly under his influence, he raises them to a height which is not natural to them, without fostering their own capacities for work at this level, so that they immediately decline again as soon as the teacher leaves the classroom. Perhaps this is how it is with me; I have sometimes thought so. (CV 38e)

## 3.3 The Significance of the Haibauer Incident (*Der Vorfall Haibauer*)[5]

In 'Time And Place For Philosophy', Cavell (2008) takes on what he calls the 'political reading' of Wittgenstein (advanced by Kripke 1982) illustrated by the so-called 'scene of instruction' in the *Investigations*, at § 217 and dismisses 'moments in Wittgenstein's biography that can seem to substantiate such a reading' by referring to 'a well-known story of his striking a pupil' where power resides purely on the side of the teacher. In contradistinction to Cavell's Romantic reading of the figure of the child and Matthews' (1994, 2005) philosophy of the child, Peters has embraced a historicist reading of Wittgenstein on the figure of the child arguing for a position that attempts to avoid both *essentializing* the child and forms of 'adultism' by historicizing subjectivity in child studies (Peters and Johansson 2012).

This argument is advanced by focusing on and exploring the biographical incident to which Cavell refers in more detail for the light it casts on Wittgenstein's teaching sensibilities and his state of mind in the period he was a teacher (especially his suicide ideation) including his relationships with the Austrian children he taught. In one sense, to anticipate an argument, the period Wittgenstein spent teaching might be usefully viewed in terms of a trope (rather than retrospective psychiatric assessment) that pictures Wittgenstein in a deeply ethical struggle to make the personal self-transformation exemplified by the shift in his work from the 'solipsism' of the *Tractatus* to the 'social being' of the *Investigation* (Fitzgerald 2004). The effect of this historicist approach is also in part to relativize Wittgenstein's teaching experience of rural village children and the discipline and punishments he administered to the cultural context of his time *circa* 1920s Austria

---

[4]Putnam (2002, 34) addresses the problem of the ethically thick concept of the 'good teacher': one who might be cruel, and yet achieve great results.

[5]Excerpt from Peters (2017).

—a time when corporeal punishment of boys and girls was part of the tradition of the drill school.

The Glöckel educational reforms of the 1920s broke with the Hapsburg disciplinarian tradition to introduce social democratic principles and socialist pedagogy. Otto Glöckel, who worked with Karl Seitz (who later became head of state) developed reforms as Under Secretary of State for Education, to make 'Red Vienna' a centre for progressive socialist pedagogy in Europe. Austro-Marxist Social Democratic reforms in education were based on three main demands:

1. Insure all students acquired knowledge appropriate to his abilities;
2. Insure for the state that the population reached a minimum educational standard;
3. Independence of the school and teachers from all classes, creeds and parties (cited in Rusinow 1978).

The Glöckel reforms also reformed teacher training of *Volksschule* (Rusinow 1978), under which Wittgenstein qualified as an elementary teacher; part of these reforms insisted on 'disciplinary procedures for teaching … on the basis of a law which corresponds to modern legal principles' alongside 'complete freedom of pedagogical method' (8). This represented a shift from the authoritarian and discipline-focused method of the Hapsburg era when physical punishments were common and the teacher's position as disciplinarian was relatively unchecked.

Wittgenstein's decision to train as a teacher had a strong vocational (in the sense of *vocation* as 'mission') and enduring spiritual basis. On the outbreak of war, Wittgenstein served in an artillery battalion and was captured. He spent over 10 months as a prisoner of war in Italy. During his war years, he pursued his work on logic writing what was to become the *Tractatus Logico-Philosophicus* which he believed provided the final solutions to philosophy. While professing not to be a religious man (in an institutional sense), 'Wittgenstein had developed an intense desire for moral and spiritual purity' (Malcolm 1995, 23). According to Malcolm (1981), Wittgenstein described himself as marginally intrigued and often moved by religion: 'I am not a religious man but I cannot help seeing every problem from a religious point of view.' He carried around Tolstoy's *The Gospels in Brief* during his war years claiming it had 'virtually kept him alive' (letter to Ficker, 24.7.15). At Cassino, Wittgenstein met Dario Antiseri and Franz Parak, both teachers, who made up a circle of friends that had formed around him to read Dostoyevsky's *Raskolnikov*. Parak (1978) writes:

> I was already a schoolteacher, and he confided to me that he also wanted to become a teacher. Obviously he believed that with his *Tractatus* he had brought his philosophical task to its end, and that now he should think about looking for a profession suited to him intellectually and morally. "In reality," he told me, "I would have preferred to become a priest, but also as a teacher I shall read the Gospel together with the children."

When released from being a prisoner of war Wittgenstein returned to Vienna, he gave away his fortune to brother and sisters and *within ten days* registered at the teachers training college in Vienna in 1919.

There is an argument for considering the years that Monk (1991) in his otherwise splendid biography calls 'Years in the Wilderness' as a *critical* episode in Wittgenstein's life determining his philosophical development, rather than 'time-out' or transitional years between early and late philosophies. The years from 1919 to 1920 when Wittgenstein attended training college in Vienna through to 1926 when he abruptly resigned from his six years teaching after an incident involving a pupil that led to a court trial constitute in many ways a central and smouldering episode in Wittgenstein's own psychological make-up, disposition and ethical self-development—one that he returns to many years later as the basis for his 'confession'. These 7 or so years spent as a teacher not only informed the development of his thinking in the *Philosophical Investigations* with an emphasis on a philosophy of language that focuses on a cultural account of learning words but also links biographically to a set of attitudes and self-dispositions that characterized Wittgenstein's unsuccessful early schooling years, his university studies leading up to his engagements with Frege and Russell, his experience as a university professor of philosophy at Cambridge including his attitude to academia and his distinctive 'styles' of thinking (Peters 2001).

In 1920, Wittgenstein took up his first position as an elementary school teacher in Trattenbach, a village of just a few hundred people. In September 1922, Wittgenstein transferred to a secondary school in Hassbach, a village nearby. A month later, he took up a position in Puchberg, a primary school in the Schneeberg mountains. In September 1924, he moved again to a school in Otterthal, near Trattenbach. In each location, he was regarded with suspicion by the villagers and made fun of by his pupils. He spoke in an aristocratic High German accent and tried to cover up his background as belonging to one of the richest families in Austria. He was partly in consequence the object of mistrust and considerable gossip. Wittgenstein regarded his pupils with contempt and often resorted to corporal punishment. He was miserable and still suffering from his experience of war and from the reception and misunderstanding of his magnum opus the *Tractatus* in which he thought he had solved all the problems of modern philosophy. He often thought of himself as worthless and a moral failure with a degree of self-criticism that verged on self-loathing and was constantly agitated and suicidal. At the same time, he was an inspiring and demanding teacher who was determined to teach the village children in his charge *everything* of which he was capable by all available means. Wittgenstein's unhappy consciousness as a schoolteacher is revealed in remarks to Russell early in his teaching career. He reports to Russel first that he is 'hopeful' and 'happy at his work' and that 'I need it badly, or else all the devils in Hell break loose inside me.' In October 1921, a year later he writes to Russell again: 'I am still at Trattenbach, surrounded, as ever, by odiousness and baseness. I know that human beings on the average are not worth much anywhere, but here they are much more good-for-nothing and irresponsible than elsewhere.' Clearly, the Tolstoyan romance of education of Austrian village children was already wearing thin. In response to Russell, he acknowledges that the 'Trattenbachers are not uniquely worse than the rest of humanity.' Somewhat later he indicates how depressed he has been 'Not that I find elementary school distasteful: quite the contrary.' He senses hopelessness in part because there is no one he can talk to. In his next position, he complains it is no better than the last and exclaims: 'Living with human beings is hard! Only they are not really human, but rather ¼ animal and ¾ human' (LRKM; see Friesen 2016).

There are a string of minor incidents where children report Wittgenstein to their parents for 'hair pulling' and 'boxing their ears.'[6] Things came to a head in April 1926 in an incident known as *Der Vorfall Haibauer*, an incident involving an 11-year-old boy, Josef Haibauer, described as a 'slow learner'. Wittgenstein reportedly hit him on the head several times and the boy collapsed unconscious. Carrying the boy to the headmaster's office, Wittgenstein bumped into Herr Piribauer, a parent whose daughter Wittgenstein had previously punished pulling her so hard by the ears that they bled. Piribauer was outraged and when he met Wittgenstein in the hall he 'called him [Wittgenstein] all the names under the sun' saying he was 'an animal trainer not a teacher' and tried to call the police to have him arrested but the office was unattended. When Piribauer tried to contact the police again next day, Wittgenstein had disappeared and he resigned from his teaching post on April 28. In May, proceedings were initiated against him and he was summoned to appear before the court. The acting judge suspecting he was mentally ill ordered a psychiatric examination of Wittgenstein. Waugh (2010, 148–9) reports that Wittgenstein lied about his ill-treatment of his pupils and that he wrote to Rudolf Koder 'I'm curious to know what the psychiatrist will say to me, but I find the idea of the examination nauseating and am heartily sick of the whole filthy business.' Proceedings continued into August but then nothing further is known about the case, the psychiatric examination or the outcome of the trial, except that it seems Wittgenstein was exonerated and went free. There is also the suggestion that the Wittgenstein family and family money had a hand in a cover-up (Waugh 2011, 149).

## 3.4 Philosophically Questioning Certainty: Distinctions Between Empirical (Causal) Inquiries and Grammatical Concerns

Wittgenstein later (c. 1950) reflected on his certainty when professing the validity of his pedagogic techniques.

> I myself wrote in my book that children learn to understand a word in such and such a way. Do I know that, or do I believe it? Why in such a case do I write not "I believe etc." but simply the indicative sentence? (OC §290)

[6]See the picture of Wittgenstein with his pupils in Puchberg am Schneeberg, circa 1922: https://en.wikipedia.org/wiki/Haidbauer_incident

Weighing grammatical suitability in applying the concept 'believing' versus 'knowing' when no doubt occurs in *the flow* of teaching: Wittgenstein distinguishes his philosophical from pedagogical remarks. Repeatedly, Wittgenstein notes that reflections on students 'taking things together' in arithmetic or learning the multiplication table are observations or 'remarks about concepts, not about teaching methods' (PI, pp. 208, 227).

> How does one teach a child (say in arithmetic) "Now take these things together!" or "Now these go together"? Clearly "taking together" and "going together" must originally have had another meaning for him than that of seeing in this way or that. – And this is a remark about concepts, not about teaching methods. (PI, p. 208)
>
> "We all learn the same multiplication table." This might, no doubt, be a remark about the teaching of arithmetic in our schools, – but also an observation about the concept of the multiplication table. (PI, p. 227)
>
> Am I doing child psychology? I am making a connexion between the concept of teaching and the concept of meaning. (Z §412)

He was philosophically concerned at Cambridge with ontological problems of meaning instead of earlier training in pedagogy. It is highly unlikely that Wittgenstein saw teaching as a legitimate 'science' (Standish 1995); his philosophical methods aver scientific approach, employing instead ethnography and attending to enculturation (Smeyers 1995, 2008).

> When I write down a bit of a series, that you then see this regularity in it may be called an empirical fact, a psychological fact. But, if you have seen this law in it, that you then continue the series in this way – that is no longer an empirical fact. (RFM VI.26; cf. PI §109)

Adumbrated here, (empirical) science and (grammatical) philosophy are like passing trains:

> The existence of the experimental method makes us think we have the means of solving the problems which trouble us; though problem and method pass one another by. (PI, xiv, p. 232).

Answering his interlocutor's accusation that emphasis on training amounts to operant conditioning, Wittgenstein again shifts attention from science to grammar.

> "Are you not really a behaviourist in disguise? Aren't you at bottom really saying that everything except human behaviour is a fiction?" – If I do speak of fiction, then it is of a grammatical fiction. (PI §307)

Not throwing out empirical studies on the basis of this distinction, Wittgenstein advised not waiting for a future science of 'mental states' to answer our questions about what makes sense philosophically or pedagogically:

> Sometime perhaps we shall know more about them – we think. But that is just what commits us to a particular way of looking at the matter. For we have a definite concept of what it means to learn to know a process better. (The decisive movement in the conjuring trick has been made, and it was the very one that we thought quite innocent.) (PI §308)

Deflating expectations, waiting for educational psychology to solve our problem of what constitutes 'sound' teaching is like anticipating 'science' to explain what is beautiful or tasteful.

> You might think Aesthetics is a science telling us what's beautiful – almost too ridiculous for words. I suppose it ought to include also what sort of coffee tastes well. (CV §2, p. 11)

Equally, however, Wittgenstein is not anti-etiological; recall that he came to Manchester to study aeronautical engineering (see Monk 1990). Demonstrating that interpretations of rules seem to 'hang in the air', unable to support or determine meaning, Wittgenstein draws an illustrative connection.

> "Then can whatever I do be brought into accord with the rule?" – Let me ask this: what has the expression of a rule – say a sign-post – got to do with my actions? What sort of connexion is there here? – Well, perhaps this one: I have been trained to react to this sign in a particular way, and now I do so react to it.
>
> But that is only to give a causal connexion; to tell how it has come about that we now go by the sign-post; not what this going-by-the-sign really consists in. On the contrary; I have further indicated that a person goes by a sign-post only in so far as there exists a regular use of sign posts, a custom. (PI §198)

His distinction shifts emphasis from etiological inquiries into learning, to inspection of training into culturally sanctioned practices and customs.

> "How am I able to obey a rule?" – If this is not a question about causes, then it is about justification for my following the rule in the way I do. (PI §217)
>
> Here we are not asking ourselves what are the causes and what produces this impression in a particular case. (PI, p. 201, on seeing something *as*, say, a triangle)

Pragmatic learning-theory as inquiry into causal processes (e.g. 'teaching by means of indirection') attends, fallibly but instrumentally, to causal learning-conditions. Contrast Dewey's interest with Wittgenstein's:

> Growth in judgment and understanding is essentially growth in ability to form purposes and to select and arrange means for their realization. The most elementary experiences of the young are filled with cases of the means-consequences relationship. …The trouble with education is not the absence of situations in which the causal relation is exemplified in the relation of means and consequences. Failure to utilize the situations so as to lead the learner on to grasp the relation in given cases of experience is, however, only too common. (Dewey 1938, 104–105)

Although Wittgenstein too appears to have been rearranging conditions to effect learning in his elementary classroom and dictionary, his later philosophical pursuit concerns how—once meaning is secured through training—it ranges 'sensibly' within our grammar. For Wittgenstein, causal relationships securing learning—an educational psychology topic of possible importance in teaching—is not a philosophical (ontological) issue, whereas degrees of arbitrariness and grammatical entanglement in educational language are ostensibly 'philosophical' (PI §§124–

126). Almost whimsically, Wittgenstein sometimes transgresses his own boundaries (recalling limit-talk in his earlier *Tractatus* and 'Lecture on Ethics'; see Ch 1)[7]:

> To say "This combination of words makes no sense" excludes it from the sphere of language and thereby bounds the domain of language. But when one draws a boundary it may be for various kinds of reason. If I surround an area with a fence or a line or otherwise, the purpose may be to prevent something from getting in or out; but it may also be part of the game and players supposed, say, to jump over the boundary; or it may shew where the property of one man ends and that of another begins; and so on. So if I draw a boundary line that is not to say what I am drawing it for. (OC §499)
>
> When a sentence is called senseless, it is not as it were its sense that is senseless. But a combination of words is being excluded from the language, withdrawn from circulation. (OC §500)

Medina (2002, 158) notes this separation from causes was made too insistently in the early 1930s, softening in Wittgenstein's thinking after 1938. Contrast, for instance, his 1930s Cambridge lectures with 1940s emphasis (*RFM* and *PI*) on training securing rules.

> The process of learning does not matter; it is history and history does not matter here. … This laying down of a rule is exactly analogous to learning language. The laying down of the rule is not contained in following the rule; the laying down is history. (WL, §2, p. 55)
>
> When we learn the meaning of a symbol the way in which we learn it is irrelevant to our future use and understanding of it. The way in which I learned my A B C and learned to read is irrelevant to my future understanding of written symbols — it is a matter of purely historical interest. But something does as it were adhere to the symbol in the process of my learning its meaning, and this becomes part of the symbol. (WL §3, p. 117)

Williams (1999, 216), explains that 'The normativity of our practices involves non-causal necessity, that is, logical or grammatical necessity.' By this curious phrase, she means to say that learning to follow directions (ostension or rule-following) presupposes a common background of what is 'obviously the same' for all participants in the learning. This common background for judgment is acquired in the process of training, or in mastering techniques, making the process of learning techniques constitutive of what is learned and enabling learners to recognize sameness, carrying on in the same way as others do.

> The schoolboy believes his teachers and his schoolbooks. (OC §263)
>
> What we believe depends on what we learn.… (OC §286)

## 3.5 Wittgenstein's Emphasis on Training

Wittgenstein's numerous remarks on 'training' support the view that linguistic, mathematical and musical practices are grafted onto our animal reactions; such second-nature 'continuations' are in themselves 'an extremely important fact of

---

[7]For how is the concept of a game bounded? …We do not know the boundaries because none have been drawn. To repeat, we can draw a boundary—for a special purpose. Does it take that to make the concept usable? Not at all! (Except for that special purpose.) (PI §§68–69)

nature' (Z §355; cf. BB, pp. 79–80, re: the same training techniques applied to animals).

> By nature and by particular training, a particular education, we are disposed to give spontaneous expression to wishes in certain circumstances. (PI §441)
>
> Being sure that someone is in pain, doubting whether he is, and so on, are so many natural, instinctive, kinds of behaviour towards other human beings, and our language is merely an auxiliary to, and further extension of, this relation. (Z §545)

Reading Wittgenstein's 'scenes of instruction' for pedagogical technique is potentially hazardous: they illustrate scaffolding needed for rule-following, giving a basis for determining rule 'accordance' (or going-against, PI §201). Here is how he depicts the familiar teaching situation of conveying a rule in mathematics, which as we suggested (in Chap. 2) cannot be contorted into something 'brutal' (as Friesen suggests generally of Wittgenstein's references to training):

> Then am I defining "order" and "rule" by means of "regularity"? – How do I explain the meaning of "regular", "uniform", "same" to anyone? – I shall explain these words to someone who, say, only speaks French by means of the corresponding French words. But if a person has not yet got the *concepts*, I shall teach him to use the words by means of *example* and by *practice*. – And when I do this I do not communicate less to him than I know myself.
>
> In the course of this teaching I shall shew him the same colours, the same lengths, the same shapes, I shall make him find them and produce them, and so on. I shall, for instance, get him to continue an ornamental pattern uniformly when told to do so. – And also to continue progressions. And so, for example, when given: ... to go on: ....
>
> I do it, he does it after me; and I influence him by expressions of agreement, rejection, expectation, encouragement. I let him go his way, or hold him back; and so on.
>
> Imagine witnessing such teaching. None of the words would be explained by means of itself; there would be no logical circle.
>
> The expressions "and so on", "and so on ad infinitum" are also explained in his teaching. A gesture that means "go on like this", or "and so on" has a function comparable to that of pointing to an object or a place.
>
> We should distinguish between the "and so on" which is, and the "and so on" which is not, an abbreviated notation. "And so on ad inf." is *not* such an abbreviation. The fact that we cannot write down all the digits of $\pi$ is not a human shortcoming, as mathematicians sometimes think. Teaching which is not meant to apply to anything but the examples given is different from that which '*points beyond*' them. (PI §208)

In subsequent sections, he gives sense to the remark (in §208 above): *And when I do this I do not communicate less to him than I know myself.* 'But then, doesn't our understanding reach beyond all the examples?'—A very queer expression, and a quite natural one!—…(PI §209). He questions as to why the teacher in this scenario should have a deeper explanation, or have more to give in the explanation.

> "But do you really explain to the other person what you yourself understand? Don't you get him to *guess* the essential thing? You give him examples, – but he has to guess their drift, to guess your intention." – Every explanation which I can give myself I give to him too. –"He guesses what I intend" would mean: various interpretations of my explanation come to his mind, and he lights on one of them. So in this case he could ask; and I could and should answer him. (PI §210)

> How can he *know* how he is to continue a pattern by himself – whatever instruction you give him? – Well, how do I know? – If that means "Have I reasons?" the answer is: my reasons will soon give out. And then I will act, without reasons. (PI §211)

When ordered to continue a series by someone who frightens me, I act 'with perfect certainty, and the lack of reasons does not trouble me' (PI §212).

Medina (2002, 159) concurs, noting that in Wittgenstein's later reflections on learning: 'He emphasizes that, through training processes, our behaviour becomes, not causally determined, but normatively structured; that is, we acquire the ability to engage in self-regulating behaviour'.

> So, for Wittgenstein, our training into techniques is more than an inductive process or a process of conditioning: it is a process of structuring behaviour until it becomes self-regulated. Learning processes of this kind endow us with more than behavioral dispositions or empirical certainties. These processes lead to the adoption of normative standards.... (Medina 2002, 159)

Addressing this normative aspect of training, Medina recalls Wittgenstein's descriptions of cajoling students during training: 'The words "right" and "wrong" are used when giving instruction in proceeding according to a rule. The word 'right' makes the pupil go on, the word 'wrong' holds him back' (RFM, VI.39; cf. Medina 2002, 164–5). Through drilling-and-instilling students acquire, blindly, the normative attitude of their mentors.

> When I obey a rule, I do not choose. I obey the rule blindly. (PI §219)

As Hunter (1985, 83) concludes from Wittgenstein's case of the deviant pupil who invents his own rules (PI §§185, 201): '...Once we have shaken loose a little from our fascination with the rule-following theory of mathematical competence, we can begin to show how large a role simply "being told" plays'. Medina (2002) notes that Wittgenstein underscores this normative compulsion: 'If I have grasped a rule I am bound in what I do further. [...] I am bound in my judgment about what is in accord with the rule and what not' (RFM, VI.27). Having internalized the rules or mastered the techniques (PI §199), teachers are in a position to offer demonstrations guiding student performance, as well as judge the suitability of the student's response (re: judging musical performance, CV 69–70e; Z §164).[8]

---

[8]From the case of the 'harried mathematics teacher':

> The instruction by insistence that seemed to be the way out of the impasse depicted in 185 suggests two important points: (i) That whatever rules the teacher may cite in pressing his case, the hard fact about him is that he is simply not prepared to brook any other continuation of the series than 1002, 1004.... He may adduce various rules in his desperation, but his colours show when the rule proves useless and he simply insists. ...(ii) What the student primarily learns is what the teacher insists on: to do it this way—this is what we do here. The practices that he learns in this way can be symbolized, and various of them can be represented in a formula that he comes to be able to use as he advances, but the bedrock of his understanding consists of those things he has simply been told (or, if he has proved recalcitrant or careless, the things that have been insisted upon or drilled into him). (Hunter 1985, 81–82)

Medina (2002, 164) notes that for Wittgenstein, the teacher must treat the child with 'courtesy', as though he/she is capable of making correct usage of the rules. 'The teacher treats the pupil's correct responses as indicative of an incipient competence and her incorrect responses as 'mistakes' (cf. RFM, VII.61). But the learner's reactions to the training are invested with normative significance only when viewed against the background of the whole rule-governed practice (cf. RFM, VII.47).

> Our children are not only given practice in calculation but are also trained to adopt a particular attitude towards a mistake in calculating.
>
> What I am saying is that mathematics is normative. But "norm: does not mean the same thing as "ideal." (RFM, VII.61)

The teacher checks and corrects the students' responses until self-correction takes over, thus normatively structuring the pupil's behaviour. But this inculcation into norms is not simply conditioning or what liberal-analytic philosophers have eloquently opposed as the 'suppression of reason'. Medina offers important qualification: that the higher goal of initiate-training is to open possibilities rather than merely fix them. Training students into normative attitudes, teachers create regularities, a 'consensus of action' leading towards mastery of techniques (PI §199); adept pupils, however, show more autonomous, self-corrective behaviour within the rules (cf. Medina 2004, 82–3).[9]

> Wittgenstein emphasizes that in order to respond appropriately to the teacher's guidance and correction, the learner needs to exhibit certain 'natural reactions'. But these natural reactions that are prerequisite for learning are not just perceptual reactions to salient features in the environment; they are interpersonal reactions oriented towards action. The learner needs to be sensitive and responsive to certain signs of approval and disapproval that are used to structure her behaviour normatively. According to Wittgenstein's enculturation view, the process of language learning is completed when the novice starts applying the learned procedures 'as a *matter of course*' (PI 238). This involves not only the establishment of a regularity in the learner's behaviour, but also the inculcation of a *normative attitude* towards how to proceed. Through repeated practice, the novice internalizes the normative standards of the linguistic community; and by the end of the learning process the novice regards the way she has been taught to go on as the only way to proceed. (Medina 2004, 83–84)

[9]Medina writes (2004, 83): Language learning is thus conceived, on Wittgenstein's view, as a process of *enculturation* or *apprenticeship*: linguistic norms are learned by being acculturated into shared practices. In the training process, the teacher, by virtue of her competence in the practice, functions as a representative of the community of practitioners; and, as such, she has a capacity and authority to bring the behaviour of the novice into harmony with the behaviour of the rule-following community. The goal of this training process is to bring the pupil into the practice, and this is achieved by effecting a 'consensus of action' between the pupil and the teacher, and hence, by the same token, between the pupil and the community of practitioners. As Wittgenstein puts it, 'instruction effects…*agreement in actions* on the part of the pupil and teacher' (RFM VI 45; my emphasis).

He continues, again emphasizing the student's gradual assumption of responsibility for learning, or in becoming more adept assuming greater autonomy within the rules absorbed through training.[10]

> Wittgenstein describes the adoption of normative standards through training with the image of the learner going 'in a circle'. He remarks that when a pupil sees how things *must* be done, 'he has gone in a circle' (RFM VI.7). The 'circle' created by the process of training into a technique consists in the following: that what the learner is trained to do becomes the criterion that defines what she is doing; that is, her activity is circularly defined by her own actions: how things must be done is defined by how things are actually done according to the learned procedure. Through training processes, the shared procedures and techniques become *second nature*. And thus they acquire normative force: when training is competed successfully, the learned procedures and techniques are not simply the causal determinants of our actions; they are rather the *reasons* why we do what we do in the way we do it. (Medina 2004, 84)

Gradually through normative training, we respond 'naturally' as most others do (PI §185). Specific techniques of training in different *language-games* lend nuance and relative 'degrees of certainty' (PI, p. 224) to words like 'prediction': e.g. anticipating moves in gymnastics routines, versus chemical reactions (PI §630). Wittgenstein reminds educators (Z §419) that we know a pupil has mastered the technique for using the word 'red' when he/she responds 'spontaneously' after seeing something we agree is red. Customarily, showing something red affirms its meaning, though calling anything 'red' doesn't make it so.

> The agreement, the harmony, of thought and reality consists in this: if I say falsely that something is *red*, then, for all that, it isn't *red*. And when I want to explain the word "*red*" to someone, in the sentence 'That is not red,' I do it by pointing to something red. (OC §429)

Wittgenstein's point is not that human agreement makes things red, but that we are taught to regard them *as* such (Z §422–32; see Ch 2).

> For I describe the language-game "Bring something red" to someone who can himself play it. Others I might at most teach it. (Relativity.) (Z §432; see Stickney 2008, re: Einstein's 'relativity')

The former elementary teacher pauses to note, however, that it would be rather silly to begin the teaching process this way with school-age children: pointing to things and saying 'That looks red' (Z §418). Infants absorb concepts from their surroundings; for instance, at an early age they come to see spoons *as* 'cutlery' (PI, p. 195). Characteristically, he distinguishes these remarks as bearing on philosophy rather than pedagogy, in this case is not dabbling in cognitive psychology.

> Am I doing child psychology? I am making a connexion between the concept of teaching and the concept of meaning. (Z §412)

---

[10]Medina, after Williams, also notes here the blindness to alternatives this training can instil, which is something we address in Ch 4 in terms of escaping pictures that enthrall us.

Philosophically, the case of learning language-games of 'red' takes us back to our grounding within a common *form of life*, and the educationally relevant processes of initiation by which we come to share such judgments. Pupils indicate uptake of immersive training by reacting appropriately and fluently, but 'this reaction, which is our guarantee of understanding, presupposes as a surrounding particular circumstances, particular forms of life and speech' (RFM, VII.47). Musing on how 'one belief hangs together with all the rest' and how it either accords or breaks with 'our whole system of verification,' he remarks:

> This system is something a human being acquires by means of observation and instruction. I intentionally do not say "learns". (OC §279)

Similarly, we pick up background context needed to interpret facial expressions and pain behaviour, but we do not explicitly learn this through formal instruction, nor can we easily impart expert judgment to others (PI, p. 227–8). Needed background for making inferences and judgments comes through tacitly in the process of instruction, rather like learning the significance of 'making a mistake' in the course/flow of normative training in mathematics (RFM VII.6). In this post-foundational epistemology, the rational, autonomous subject of Enlightenment and Analytic philosophy is re-immersed in the 'flow of life', where background and training set the stage for meaning.

> What determines our judgment, our concepts and reactions, is not what one man is doing now, an individual action, but the whole hurly-burly of human actions, the background against which we see any action. (Z §567–69; see Ch 2)

Sharing a *form of life* means being socialized into accepting certain customs or commands (PI §206; PI, p. 226), giving us also shared 'agreement in judgments' (PI §§241–2) upon which we can also challenge and advance claims: including the suitability of explanations delivered in the course of teaching.

> Instead of the unanalysable, specific, indefinable: the fact that we act in such-and-such ways, e.g., punish certain actions, establish the state of affairs thus and so, give orders, render accounts, describe colours, take an interest in others' feelings. What has to be accepted, the given – it might be said – are facts of living // forms of life. (PI §630; cf. PI, p. 226)

Much as we are trained to see a fork *as* cutlery (PI, p. 194–5), we come to see the world around us *as* it is mediated by the grammar of our language. Our habituation in language is what Wittgenstein alludes to through his rich concept of *forms of life*: 'To imagine a language is to imagine a form of life' (PI §19). Taylor (1995, 9, 21–23, 25, 72–73) notes that this is a Kantian argument form,[11] but whereas Kant argued that our internal (*synthetic a priori*) concepts of space, time, motion, solidity and cause and effect combine with sensations (perception and experience) to give us

[11]Or as Garver (1994) notes, it gives us a *first philosophy* or basis on which to build an otherwise post-foundational philosophy.

an epistemological fusion of rationalism and empiricism, for Wittgenstein the *a priori* is not internal or rational but grounded in shared, public or social practice.

> They are determined by a consensus of action: a consensus of doing the same thing, of reacting in the same way. There is a consensus but it is not a consensus of opinion. We all act the same way, walk the same way, count the same way. (LFM, XIX, pp. 183–84)

We see his earlier thinking on mathematics-training (1939) culminate in Wittgenstein's rule-following sequence in the *Investigations*:

> "So you are saying that human agreement decides about what is true and what is false?" – It is what human beings *say* that is true and false; and they agree in the *language* they use. That is not agreement in opinions but in forms of life. (PI §241)

> If language is to be a means of communication there must be agreement not only in definitions but also (queer as this may sound) in judgments. (PI §242)

This shared understanding is a part of our evolving 'natural history' and *form of life* (cf. PI, p. 226–8 and 230), which is why (PI, p. 229): 'A child has much to learn before it can pretend. (A dog cannot be a hypocrite, but neither can he be sincere.)' In PI §250 he ponders: 'Could one teach a dog to simulate pain?'[12] *On Certainty* again shows our ability to read pretense in facial expressions, our shared 'certainty in judgments', to be something more 'animal' than rational (see Standish 2017; Stickney 2008).

> Now I would like to regard the certainty not as something akin to hastiness or superficiality, but as a form of life. (That is badly expressed and probably badly thought as well.) (OC§358)

> But that means that I want to conceive it as something that lies beyond being justified or unjustified; as it were, as something animal. (OC §359)

> I want to regard man here as an animal; as a primitive being to which one grants instinct but not ratiocination. As a creature in a primitive state. (OC §475)

> We do not learn the practice of making empirical judgments by learning rules: we are taught *judgments* and their connexion with other judgments. A *totality* of judgments is made plausible to us. (OC §140)

For Wittgenstein (as well as Heidegger, Ponty and Foucault), it is the grammar of our language (its *as-structure*, as Mulhall 1990 describes it) that construes or discursively makes up how we see or regard things and people (including our pupils). Wittgenstein's project here as Mulhall shows (1990, 2001) is a continuation of Heidegger's reconstruction of Western ontology in *Being and Time*, freeing us from the enthralling pictures of Plato's essentialism and Descartes' subject–object duality.

> Like everything metaphysical the harmony between thought and reality is to be found in the grammar of the language. (PG, p. 161; cf. PI §§371–373).

> Essence is expressed by grammar. (PI §371)

---

[12]'If a lion could talk, we could not understand him.' (PI II, p. 223)

> Here we see that the idea of 'agreement with reality' does not have any clear application. (OC §§214–215)

Frequent scenes of training in the *Investigations*, we have argued, are not to be taken as Wittgenstein's 'guide to pedagogy'. By contrast to training, Wittgenstein's teaching style at Cambridge was a dialogical exercise in critical thinking through problem solving (see Chaps. 1 and 2).

> I should not like my writing to spare other people the trouble of thinking. (PI, viii; cf. CV 61).

Exchanging and critiquing ideas, however, presupposes commonly held, normatively enforced linguistic and mathematical practices acquired through rudimentary training (PI §§5–6; see Smeyers 2017). 'It is essential for communication that we agree in a large number of judgments' (RFM VI.39). Instead of closing space for contestation, training establishes its possibility: pre-conditional avenues for later self-regulation and improvization within-and-against the rules (PI §201), or customs for our *way of life*.

## 3.6 Reading Wittgenstein as a 'Pedagogical Philosopher': Signature Themes[13]

Over many years now, Michael Peters has joined with James Marshall, Paul Smeyers and Nicholas Burbules in advancing a reading of Wittgenstein that sees him as a 'pedagogical philosopher' instead of a 'philosopher of education' in the more overt ways of thinkers such as Locke, Rousseau Kant and Dewey (Peters 1995; Peters and Marshall 1999; Peters et al. 2008). Among many others, Stickney (2005) endorsed this reading as it resituates the discussion in a way that is healthy or therapeutic for educationists who, in reading Wittgenstein's many references to training and teaching, may be tempted to extract from his *Philosophical Investigations* a pedagogical theory or creed. This brief synopsis, familiar to some readers within the narrower discipline of Philosophy of Education, is designed to introduce the man and his work through a reading that emphasizes a broadly cultural approach to his intellectual background, context and life, recording the influence his thought has exerted on the disciplines, including education and pedagogy (see Peters 2001, 2002). Making the case for reading Wittgenstein as a 'pedagogical philosopher' points to a non-foundational approach to traditional philosophical problems: one that does not proceed by trying to discover essences or eternal forms but rather progresses through commanding a clear view of our concepts and by raising interesting questions. It is therefore an approach that deviates from the foundations of modern philosophy in that it does not based itself on the *cogito*, in the individual thinking and insofar as it avoids this centred Cartesian

---

[13]Excerpt from Stickney and Peters (2017).

figure of the subject and of subjectivity the approach adopts an anti-foundationalist stance, an anti-epistemological standpoint and entertains a suspicion of transcendental arguments preferring instead to accept a naturalism grounded in culture and social convention—in what we do and what we say.

Most recently (Peters and Stickney 2018), we have argued that Wittgenstein is not so much a philosopher who provides a method for analysing educational concepts but rather one who approaches philosophical questions from a pedagogical point of view. The analytic impulse to want to extract a theory or method from Wittgenstein or to use his method to clarify concepts in the manner of R. S. Peters is only one way of viewing the educational significance of Wittgenstein's philosophy. Perhaps more importantly, his styles are *essentially pedagogical*: he provides pictures, drawings, analogies, similes, jokes, equations, dialogues with himself, questions and wrong answers, experiments and so on, as a means to shift our thinking, to help us escape the picture that holds us captive. In this regard, it is also possible to see connections between other aspects of Wittgenstein's life, his cultural orientation and his styles of philosophizing including for example, his interest in architecture and his preference for certain musical and poetic styles and forms.

Wittgenstein's later writing is dialogical, but not in the Socratic sense: the aim is not the search for an adequate definition of a concept. Indeed, if we keep in mind the multiplicity of language-games we will not be inclined to ask questions like 'What is the meaning of…?' (PI §24). Moreover, the kinds of questions Wittgenstein asks, and the way he asks them, are different from those of Socrates. Fann (1969, 109) notes that Wittgenstein asks himself (and his readers) in the order of eight hundred questions in the *Investigations*, yet he only answers one hundred of them and of these the majority (some seventy) wrongly. If a dialogical work, the Investigations is not a conventional dialogical work, for Wittgenstein—by asking questions and answering them wrongly (deliberately)—wants to stop us from asking certain kinds of questions: the sort of 'philosophical' questions which require that we provide a theoretical answer abstracted from the context of use and social practice. Philosophy does not make progress because 'our language has remained the same and keeps seducing us into asking the same questions' (Wittgenstein, CV 15e). Moreover, the questions Wittgenstein asks are frequently posed by an imaginary interlocutor *to himself*—linking his approach again with a confessional mode in which the primary dynamic is of an inner dialogue (Finch 1995, 76).

Wittgenstein's mode of dialogue, then, is not one of *demonstration* (as it often was for Plato) but of *investigation*. Wittgenstein's use of imagined interchanges, thought-experiments and frequently cryptic aphorisms were meant to engage the reader in a process that was, in Wittgenstein's actual teaching as well as in his writing, the externalization of his own doubts, his own questions, his own thought processes. Hence, his philosophical purpose was manifested, shown, in *how* he pursued a question; his style was his method, and his writings sought to exemplify how it worked. His concern with matters of composition and form were not only about the presentation of an argument, but about the juxtaposition that would best draw the reader into the very state of puzzlement he himself felt. Therefore, an appreciation of Wittgenstein's style leads us directly to an understanding of the fundamentally *pedagogical* dimension of his philosophy.

Engelmann (1967, 114), in his memoir of Wittgenstein, warns us not to underestimate the influence of Wittgenstein's teaching experience on his philosophical works. Wittgenstein, Engelmann maintains, 'used the acquired art of asking questions with consummate skill, and the crucial simplicity with which he accomplished this in his most profound mental probings constitutes his great new philosophical achievement' (p. 115). Engelmann suggests that Wittgenstein moved to the Socratic form of questions in his later work in order to correct the reflective monologue of the *Tractatus* which were written in the form of categorical propositions.

There is more than a family resemblance between Wittgenstein's styles of teaching at Cambridge and his styles of philosophizing. They represent to all intents and purposes a profound and complex continuity: the dividing line between Wittgenstein's teachings and his posthumously collected and edited works are blurred to say the least. The oral performance runs into and sometimes constitutes the written corpus. Many of his 'works' are transcriptions, discussions, notes or lectures recorded by his students and colleagues. His 'notes', at another level of composition, are sometimes reworked even in the process of dictation. His styles of teaching and thinking in performance, therefore, comprise, perhaps more than any modern philosopher, a significant proportion of his extant works.

The accounts of his teaching by his students (see Ch 1) confirm an *intensity* of thinking that shows itself in his writings; this intensity is driven, in large part, by the ethical and aesthetic requirements of *arranging* or composing his thoughts. His writings mirror his approach to teaching philosophy and vice versa. Above all, they reflect his *honesty* as a thinker and teacher. And if he was unforgiving in his treatment of his students, it is because he was unforgiving with himself. The long painful silences that interspersed his classes, his disregard for institutional conventions in pedagogy at the time and his relentless (self) criticism were an essential part of his style as a 'great educator' (in Nietzsche's sense).

Janik and Toulmin's (1973) *Wittgenstein's Vienna* was the first to demonstrate the significance of a historico-cultural approach to understanding Wittgenstein and the importance of the Viennese cultural milieu to understanding his work. Adopting a Kantian interpretation of the early Wittgenstein, they argued he was addressing the problem of representation, a problem that arose in the culture of Viennese modernism. Janik and Toulmin argued that Wittgenstein was extending in his own way the critique of language and culture initiated by Karl Kraus (and Fritz Mauthner) and they emphasized a romantic and ethical interpretation of the *Tractatus* where, as they assert, 'Only art can express moral truth, and only the artist can teach the things that matter most in life' (Janik and Toulmin 1973, 197).

Janik (1981, 85) identifies Wittgenstein with the spirit of the Austrian counter-enlightenment characterized by a focus upon the limits of reason, in the tradition of Lichtenberg, Kraus, Schopenhauer, Kierkegaard, Weininger and Nietzsche. Von

Wright (1982), in an influential essay, argues that Wittgenstein displays a Spenglerian attitude to his times: Wittgenstein understood himself to be living in 'an age without culture', an age where modern philosophy was no longer able to provide the metalanguage which united the family resemblances of culture's various manifestations. Heller (1988) suggests that Wittgenstein in many respects resembled Nietzsche:

> in his homelessness, his restless wanderings, his perpetual search for exactly the right conditions in which to work, his loneliness, his ascetism, his need for affection and his shyness in giving it, his intellectual extremism, which drove thought to the borders of insanity, the elasticity of his style, and … in one philosophically most important respect. Like Nietzsche he knew that philosophical opinion was not merely a matter of logically demonstrable right or wrong … it was above all a matter of authenticity … (Heller 1988, 143–4).

Cavell (1988) views Wittgenstein as a 'philosopher of culture' and provides a reading of the *Investigations* as a depiction of our times, agreeing with von Wright's assessment of Wittgenstein's attitude as Spenglerian suggesting that Spengler's vision of culture as a kind of Nature is shared in a modified form in the *Investigations*. Cavell (1988, 261–2) argues that the *Investigations* 'diurnalizes Spengler's vision of the destiny toward exhausted forms', towards the loss of culture and community. Cavell draws our attention to the way Wittgenstein's uniqueness as a philosopher of culture comes from 'the sense that he is joining the fate of philosophy as such with that of the philosophy of culture or criticism of culture'. By doing so, he argues, Wittgenstein is calling into question philosopohy's claim to a privileged perspective on culture that could be called the perspective of reason.

In line with this reading, Wittgenstein's work, broadly speaking, may be given a cultural and literary reading which focuses upon his *styles*. Such a reading legitimates both the importance of Wittgenstein—the person—and the significance of his (auto)biography in a way that analytic philosophers might find hard to accept. The question of style is a question inseparable from the reality of his life and the corpus of his work. Wittgenstein himself actively thought this to be the case and that this belief is *shown* in his work. This reading also throws into relief questions concerning his appropriation as a philosopher who had something to contribute to education: Wittgenstein not as a philosopher who provides a *method* for analysing educational concepts but rather as one who approaches philosophical questions from a *pedagogical* point of view. *Wittgenstein style of 'doing' philosophy is pedagogical.* His style is *pedagogical*; he provides a teaming variety and vital repertoire of non-argumentational discursive forms—pictures, drawings, analogies, similes, jokes, equations, dialogues with himself, little narratives, questions and *wrong* answers, thought-experiments, gnomic aphorisms and so on—as a means primarily to shift our thinking, to help us escape the picture that holds us captive. It is this notion of *philosophy as pedagogy* that is a defining feature of Wittgenstein's later thought.

It is significant that for Wittgenstein in *On Certainty* (1969) language is not the foundation—words and justifications come to an end (OC §192) on the base of 'hinge propositions' which are neither true or false but 'remain firm' for us. When Wittgenstein writes: "Giving grounds, however, justifying the evidence, comes to an end; - but the end is not certain propositions' striking us immediately as true, i.e. it is not a kind of seeing on our part; it is our acting, which lies at the bottom of the language-game" (OC §204). Wittgenstein is suggesting that there is only cultural practice at the bottom of our language-games, an ungrounded way of acting. Contrary to Descartes' starting point of the indubitability of the self-reflecting *cogito* as offering the foundations of knowledge based on a mathematical model of certainty that ultimately leads to a self-stultifying solipsistic self, Wittgenstein both naturalizes and socializes cognitive processes locating them first in language and then as part of the activity of a culture. He is thus not a foundationalist in any accepted definition of the term. For him, certainty and the very possibility of meaning lies in the background context without which propositions could not even be enunciated: '…I want to conceive [certainty] as something that lies beyond being justified or unjustified; as it were, as something animal' (OC §359).

The notion of philosophy as a kind of therapy (see Semeyers et al. 2006) has a set of link and references that take us back to the beginnings of philosophy and certainly to the Stoics who held 'that emotions like fear or envy (or impassioned sexual attachments, or passionate love of anything whatsoever) either were, or arose from, false judgements and that the sage—a person who had attained moral and intellectual perfection—would not undergo them' (Baltzly 2014). The therapeutic notion of philosophy was intimately tied to the pursuit of the good life and philosophy as a therapy of emotions. Gordon Baker, among others, provides a therapeutic reading of *Investigations* that positions Wittgenstein as attempting to break us free of the impulse to metaphysics through an elaborately structured dialogue where the reader is encouraged to think for himself or herself. The work of Stanley Cavell, James Conant, and Cora Diamond regards Wittgenstein's philosophy as entirely therapeutic, rather than as having any theoretical or metaphysical aspects. Certainly, there are a range of comments by Wittgenstein scattered throughout his work where he uses the notion of therapy to describe his activity of doing philosophy such as 'In philosophizing we may not terminate a disease of thought. It must run its natural course, and slow cure is all important' (Z 1967, §382). Wittgenstein also extends this conception to education when he says 'I trot out all the problems that education represses without solving. I say to those repressed doubts: you are quite correct, go on asking, demand clarification' (PG 1974, p. 382). The justification of R. S. Peters' approach to philosophy of education by means of a distinctive and foundational method of conceptual analysis does not hold water and its justification cannot be found in Wittgenstein.

By contrast, the 'new Wittgenstein' coalesces around a series of common interpretive protocols: Wittgenstein is not advancing theories in philosophy but rather employing a therapeutic method to deconstruct philosophical puzzles; he is helping us to work free of the conceptual confusions that become evident when we begin to philosophize; at the same time, Wittgenstein is disabusing us of the notion that we can stand outside language and command an external view, and that such an external view is both necessary and possible for grasping the essence of thought and language. On the new reading, Wittgenstein encourages us to see that our intuitions about meaning and thought are best accommodated 'by attention to our everyday forms of expression and to the world those forms of expression serve to reveal' (Crary and Read 2000, 1). This new schema for reading Wittgenstein puts less emphasis on the decisive break in his thought, represented by the *Tractatus* and the posthumous *Investigations*, to emphasize, by comparison, significant continuities of his thought centring around his therapeutic conception of philosophy. The new reading that emphasizes the therapeutic character of Wittgenstein's philosophical aims and method is sympathetic to and consistent with the 'postmodern' view of Wittgenstein (Peters and Marshall 1999) which explicitly provides an emphasis on a literary, cultural and (auto)biographical reading of Wittgenstein's works, their intertextuality, the expression of the spirit of European (Viennese) modernism in the *Tractatus*, and the anticipation of certain 'postmodern' themes in his later works which, on the one hand, cast him in close philosophical proximity to Schopenhauer, Nietzsche and Heidegger and, on the other, project his writings into an interesting engagement with poststructuralist thought (Peters and Marshall 1999, 19–20).

This cultural reading, in part, was inspired by Cavell's work, which serves as an exemplar both in reading Wittgenstein in relation to the movement of *modernism* and against Wittgenstein's Viennese cultural background where the influence of Nietzsche, Schopenhauer and Freud is evident. Cavell's writings draw widely upon the philosophical tradition and emphasize the parallels between Wittgenstein and many contemporary thinkers, including both Derrida and Foucault. It is a view that sits well with Wittgenstein as a pedagogical philosopher (Peters et al. 2008/2010).[14] In the 'postmodern' reading, the *Tractatus* is seen to be *modernist in its formalism*, while the *Investigations* anticipates certain 'postmodernist' themes including anti-foundationalism and anti-representationalism (Peters and Marshall 1999). The distinction is principally a matter of the style of *doing* philosophy and it is reflective of the impact of larger cultural forces upon Wittgenstein and, significantly, also the 7 years Wittgenstein as an elementary schoolteacher in rural Austria. It does not deny that there are significant continuities in his thought, say, for instance in his view of philosophy. In this reading, it is possible to argue that the therapeutic aim became more manifest in Wittgenstein's 'pedagogical' style and in a view called 'philosophy as pedagogy' (Peters and Marshall 1999). This view does not entail necessarily an account of 'social constructivism', or imply that 'postmodernism' (whatever that elusive term means) necessarily entails social constructivism in any of its versions. In one sense, 'post-foundational' is a better term that serves to provide a general philosophical direction in epistemology, learning and ethics.

The cultural and postmodern reading of Wittgenstein, like much of postmodernism, considered as a whole, tends to emphasize a number of overlapping cluster

[14]Contra R. S. Peters' (1965) misreading of Wittgenstein: another enthralling picture (see Peters and Stickney 2018).

concepts that emphasize its openness and lack of essentiality, including the following:

- anti-foundationalism;
- anti-essentialism;
- anti- or post-epistemological standpoint;
- anti-realism about meaning and reference;
- suspicion of transcendental arguments and viewpoints;
- rejection of the picture of knowledge as accurate representation;
- rejection of truth as correspondence to reality;
- rejection of canonical descriptions and final vocabularies;
- suspicion of metanarratives.

The list is taken from Magnus' (1989) discussion of Nietzsche in relation to postmodern criticism. To Magnus' list, it is relevant to add what Rorty (1979) calls 'anti-representationalism' and also to add, alongside 'suspicion of metanarratives,' the turn to narrative and narratology, more generally—*petite récits* pitted against metanarratives by Lyotard (1984) who significantly, makes central use of Wittgenstein in a creative misappropriation to emphasize the conflictual or dissensual, nature of language-games (cf. Burbules 2000). We might add an emphasis on linguistic use and *therapeutic view of philosophy*—that is, an embodiment of many of the features of the list above and an ethos, above all, concerning philosophy as a critique of language summed up best in the famous quotation from the *Investigations*: 'Philosophy is a battle against the bewitchment of our intelligence by means of language' (PI §109). This is a view that underlies the development of social sciences and cultural studies in the latter half of the twentieth-century; perhaps, sloganized in the twin methodological imperatives: the linguistic turn, the significance of representation, and turn to social practices, on the one hand; and, the attempt to overcome the dualistic thought, the search for certainty and essences and the subjectivism that are the legacies of the Cartesian thought, on the other. Encouraged by Wittgenstein's expert disassembly of the Cartesian worldview and model of subjectivity, we might entertain a model of education as openness, engagement and *co-poiesis*, one that is more suited to the global, networked and digital environment we live in.

## References

Baltzly, D. (2014). "Stoicism". In E. N. Zalta (Ed.), *The Stanford encyclopedia of philosophy* (Spring Edition). http://plato.stanford.edu/archives/spr2014/entries/stoicism/.

Bartley, W. W., III. (1974). Theory of language and philosophy of science as instruments of educational reform: Wittgenstein and Popper as Austrian schoolteachers. In R. S. Cohen & W. W. Wartofsky (Eds.), *Methodological and historical studies in the natural social sciences* (pp. 207–337)., Boston Studies in the Philosophy of Science. XIV Boston: D. Reidel.

Bartley, W. W., III. (1985). *Wittgenstein* (2d ed.). LaSalle, IL: Open Court.

Burbules, N. (2000). Lyotard on Wittgenstein. In P. A. Dhillon & P. Standish (Eds.), *Lyotard. Just education*. London and New York: Routledge.
Cavell, S. (1988). *Declining decline: Wittgenstein as a philosopher of culture. Inquiry, 31*(3), 253–264.
Cavell, S. (2008). Time and place for philosophy. *Metaphilosophy, 39*(1), 51–61.
Crary, A., & Read, R. J. (Eds.). (2000). *The new Wittgenstein*. London: Routledge.
Dewey, J. (1938). *Experience and education*. New York: Collier Books. In: *John Dewey: The Later Works*, vol. 12. Carbondale: Southern Illinois University Press, 1991.
Edmonds, D., & Eidnow, J. (2001). *Wittgenstein's poker. The story of a ten-minute argument between two great philosophers*. London: Faber & Faber.
Engelmann, P. (1967). *Letters from Ludwig Wittgenstein* (L. Furtmuller, Trans.). Oxford: Basil Blackwell.
Fann, K. T. (1969). *Wittgenstein's conception of philosophy*. Oxford: Basil Blackwell.
Finch, H. L. (1995). *Wittgenstein (The spirit of philosophy)*. Dorset, UK: Element.
Fitzgerald, M. (2004). *Autism and creativity: Is there a link between autism in men and exceptional ability?* New York: Routledge.
Friesen, N. (2016). Lost in translation: Ludwig Wittgenstein, education and the question of *abrichtung*. Presented at the *Philosophy of Education Society* annual meeting, Toronto, 2016; also found at http://blogs.ubc.ca/nfriesen/files/2015/08/wittgenstein-training.pdf.
Fuller, S. (2004). *Kuhn vs. Popper: The struggle for the soul of science*. Thriplow, UK and New York: Icon Books, Columbia University Press.
Garver, N. (1994). *This complicated form of life. Essays on Wittgenstein*. Chicago and Lasalle, IL: Open Court.
Hargrove, E. C. (1980). Wittgenstein, Bartley, and the Glöckel school reform. *Journal of the History of Philosophy, 18*(4), 453–461.
Heller, Erich. (1988). Wittgenstein and Nietzsche . In *The importance of Nietzsche*, (Ch 8). Chicago: University of Chicago Press.
Hunter, J. F. M. (1985). The Harried mathematics instructor. In *Understanding Wittgenstein: Studies of philosophical investigations*. Edinburgh: Edinburgh University Press.
Janik, A. (1981). Wittgenstein, an Austrian enigma. In J. K. Nyíri (Ed.), *Austrian philosophy: Studies and texts*. Philosophia-Verlag.
Janik, A., & Toulmin, S. (1973). *Wittgenstein's Vienna*. New York: Simon & Schuster.
Kripke, S. (1982). The Wittgensteinian paradox. In *Wittgenstein on rules and private language. An elementary exposition*. Oxford: Basil Blackwell.
Lyotard, J-F. (1984). *The postmodern condition: A report on knowledge*. (G. Bennington and B. Massumi; Foreword F. Jameson Trans.). Manchester: Manchester University Press.
Magnus, B. (1989). Nietzsche and postmodern criticism. *Nietzsche-Studien, 18*(December), 301–316.
Malcolm, N. (1981). Wittgenstein's confessions. *London Review of Books, 3*(21).
Malcolm, N. (1995). In: P. Winch (Ed.), *Wittgenstein: A religious point of view*. Ithaca, NY: Cornell University Press.
Matthews, G. (1994). *The philosophy of childhood*. Cambridge, MA: Harvard University Press.
Matthews, G. (2005). The philosophy of childhood. *The Stanford encyclopedia of philosophy*. http://plato.stanford.edu/entries/childhood/.
Medina, J. (2002). *The unity of Wittgenstein's philosophy. Necessity, intelligibility, and normativity*. Albany: State University of New York Press.
Medina, J. (2004). Wittgenstein's social naturalism: The idea of '*second nature*'. In D. Moyal-Sharrock (Ed.), *The third Wittgenstein: The post-investigation works*. Aldershot: Ashgate.
Monk, R. (1990). *Ludwig Wittgenstein: The duty of genius*. London: Vintage.
Monk, R. (1991). *Wittgenstein: The duty of genius*. London: Penguin Books.
Mulhall, S. (1990). *On being in the world. Wittgenstein and Heidegger on seeing aspects*. London and New York: Routledge.

Mulhall, S. (2001). Seeing aspects. In H.-J. Glock (Ed.), *Wittgenstein. A critical reader.* Oxford: Blackwell.
Parak, F. (1978). *Selections from Wittgenstein prigioniero a Cassino* (Roma 1978; R.W. Angelo Trans. ). At http://www.roangelo.net/logwitt/acassino.html.
Peters, M. A. (1995). Philosophy and education: 'After' Wittgenstein. In J. Marshall & P. Smeyers (Eds.), *Philosophy and education: Accepting Wittgenstein's challenge* (pp. 189–204). Dordrecht, Boston and London: Kluwer Academic Publishers.
Peters, M. A. (2001). Philosophy as pedagogy: Wittgenstein's styles of thinking. *Radical Pedagogy*, 3(3). http://radicalpedagogy.icaap.org/content/issue3_3/4-peters.html#1.
Peters, M. A. (2002). Writing the self: Wittgenstein, confession and pedagogy. *Journal of Philosophy of Education, 34*(2), 353–368.
Peters, M. A. (2017). Wittgenstein's trials, teaching and Cavell's romantic "figure of the child". In M. A. Peters & J. Stickney (Eds.), *A companion to Wittgenstein on education: Pedagogical investigations* (pp. 211–230). Singapore: Springer.
Peters, M. A., Burbules, N., & Smeyers, P. (2008). *Showing and doing: Wittgenstein as a pedagogical philosopher*. London: Routledge.
Peters, M. A, & Johansson, V. (2012). *Historizing subjectivity in childhood studies, linguistic and philosophical investigations* (Vol. 11, pp. 42–61).
Peters, M. A., & Marshall, J. (1999). *Wittgenstein: Philosophy, postmodernism, pedagogy*. Westport, CT and London: Bergin and Garvey.
Peters, M. A., & Stickney, J. (2018, in press). Philosophy of education 1945–2010 and the 'education of reason': Post-foundational approaches through Dewey, Wittgenstein, and Foucault. In K. Becker & I. Thomson (Eds.), *The Cambridge history of philosophy, 1945–2015*. Cambridge: Cambridge University Press.
Peters, R. S. (1965). Education as initiation. In R. D. Archamabult (Ed.), *Philosophical analysis and education* (pp. 87–111). New York: The Humanities Press.
Philips, D. L. (1977). *Wittgenstein and scientific knowledge: A sociological perspective*. Totowa, NJ: Rowan and Littlefield.
Putnam, H. (2002). *The collapse of the fact/value dichotomy and other essays*. Cambridge, MA and London: Harvard University Press.
Rhees, R. (Ed.). (1981). *Ludwig Wittgenstein: Personal recollections*. Oxford: Blackwell.
Rorty, R. (1979). *Philosophy and the mirror of nature*. Princeton: Princeton University Press.
Rusinow, D. (1978). *Otto Glockel and Austrian school reform movement*. At http://www.icwa.org/wp-content/uploads/2015/09/DR-65.pdf.
Savickey, B. (1999). *Wittgenstein's art of investigation*. London and New York: Routledge.
Savickey, B. (2017). Wittgenstein's philosophy: *Viva voce*. In M. A. Peters & J. Stickney (Eds.), *A companion to Wittgenstein on education: Pedagogical investigations* (pp. 63–78). Singapore: Springer.
Smeyers, P. (1995). Initiation and newness in education and childrearing. In J. Marshall & P. Smeyers (Eds.), *Philosophy and education: Accepting Wittgenstein's challenge* (pp. 105–126). Dordrecht, Boston and London: Kluwer Academic Publishers.
Smeyers, P. (2008). Images and pictures: Seeing and imagining. In M. A. Peters, N. Burbules, & P. Smeyers (Eds.), *Saying and doing: Wittgenstein as a pedagogical philosopher (Ch 4)*. Boulder: Paradigm Press.
Smeyers, P. (2017). "This is simply what I do." On the relevance of Wittgenstein's alleged conservatism and the debate about Cavell's legacy for children and grown-ups. In M. A. Peters, & J. Stickney (Eds.), *A companion to Wittgenstein on education: Pedagogical investigations* (pp. 241–259). Singapore: Springer.
Smeyers, P., Smith, R., & Standish, P. (2006). *The therapy of education*. Basingstoke: Palgrave Macmillan.
Standish, P. (1995). Why we should not speak of an educational science. In J. Marshall & P. Smeyers (Eds.), *Philosophy and education: Accepting Wittgenstein's challenge* (pp. 143–158). Dordrecht, Boston and London: Kluwer Academic Publishers.

Standish, P. (2017). Something animal? Wittgenstein, language, instinct. In M. A. Peters & J. Stickney (Eds.), *A companion to Wittgenstein on education: Pedagogical investigations* (pp. 261–274). Singapore: Springer.

Stickney, J. (2005). Teaching and learning in Wittgenstein's philosophic method. In K. Howe (Ed.), *Philosophy of education society yearbook, 2005* (pp. 299–308). Paper given at the PES annual meeting, San Francisco.

Stickney, J. (2008). Wittgenstein's 'relativity': Agreement in *forms of life* and training in language-games. In N. Burbules & P. Smeyers (Guest Eds.); M. A. Peters, (Ed.). Special edition on Wittgenstein (September). *Educational Philosophy and Theory*, 40(5).

Stickney, J. (2017). Wittgenstein as educator. In M. A. Peters & J. Stickney (Eds.), *A companion to Wittgenstein on education: Pedagogical investigations*, 43–62. Singapore: Springer.

Stickney, J., & Peters, M. A. (2017). Journeys with Wittgenstein: Assembling sketches of a philosophical landscape. In M. A. Peters & J. Stickney (Eds.), *A companion to Wittgenstein on education: Pedagogical investigations* (pp. 3–28). Singapore: Springer.

Taylor, C. (1995). *Philosophical arguments*. Cambridge, MA: Harvard University Press.

Von Wright, G. H. (1982). Wittgenstein in relation to his time. In A. Kenny and B. McGuinness (Eds.), *Wittgenstein and his times*. Chicago: University of Chicago Press.

Waugh, A. (2010). *The house of Wittgenstein: A family at war*. New York: Anchor.

Waugh, A. (2011). *The house of Wittgenstein: A family at war*. New York: Anchor.

Williams, M. (1999). The etiology of the obvious. Wittgenstein and the elimination of indeterminacy. In *Wittgenstein, mind and meaning. Toward a social conception of mind* (Ch 8). London and New York: Routledge.

Wittgenstein, L. (1956). *Remarks on the foundation of mathematics* (G. E. M. Anscombe, Trans.). Oxford: Basil Blackwell (RFM).

Wittgenstein, L. (1961). *Notebooks 1914–1916* (G. E. M. Anscombe, Trans.). New York (N): Harper.

Wittgenstein, L. (1967). *Zettel* (G. E. M. Anscombe, Trans.). Oxford: Basil Blackwell (Z).

Wittgenstein, L. (1968). *Philosophical investigations* (3d ed.) (G. E. M. Anscombe, Trans.). Oxford: Basil Blackwell (PI§, or PI, pg.).

Wittgenstein, L. (1969a). *The blue and brown books: Preliminary studies for the 'Philosophical investigations'*. Oxford: Basil Blackwell (BB).

Wittgenstein, L. (1969). *On certainty* (D. Paul & G. E. M. Anscombe, Trans.). Oxford: Basil Blackwell (OC).

Wittgenstein, L. (1974). *Letters to Russell, Keynes and Moore* (G. H. von Wright assisted by B. F. McGuinness, Eds.). Oxford: Basil Blackwell (LRKM).

Wittgenstein, L. (1974). *Philosophical grammar*. R. Rhees (Ed.), A. Kenny (Trans.). Oxford: Blackwell.

Wittgenstein, L. (1979). In A. Ambrose (Ed.), *Wittgenstein's lectures, Cambridge, 1932–35*. Oxford: Blackwell (WL).

Wittgenstein, L. (1980). *Culture and value*. G.H. von Wright (Ed.) in collaboration with H. Nyman. P. Winch (Trans.). Oxford: Basil Blackwell (CV).

Wittgenstein, L. (1993). *Philosophical occasions (1912–1951)*. J. C. Klagge & A. Nordmann (Ed.). Indianapolis and Cambridge: Hackett (PO).

# Chapter 4
# Pedagogical Investigations

> A man will be *imprisoned* in a room with a door that's unlooked and opens inwards; as long as it does not occur to him to *pull* rather push it. (CV 42e)[1]
>
> If we look at things from an ethnological point of view, does that mean that we are saying that philosophy is ethnology? No, it only means that we are taking up a position right outside so as to be able to see things *more objectively*. (CV 37e)

## 4.1 Recontextualizing Wittgenstein's Cases of Training and Learning[2]

Wittgenstein's 6-year experience as an elementary teacher may provide a reason for dwelling on pupils and learning; it tells us little, however, about the role this plays in his philosophy. Biographical approaches often aim at a second-order, causal explanation (see Ch 1 and 3), whereas Wittgenstein exhorts us to describe usage, 'in such a way as to make us recognize those workings: *in despite of* an urge to misunderstand them' (PI §109). His philosophical task was to shift the *pivotal interest* of our investigation: 'the axis of reference of our examination must be rotated, but about the fixed point of our real need' (PI §108). O*ur* need here is to see that simplified learning practices occasion philosophical investigations; they give us a perspicuous view of how pupils come to play, and later contest, certain *language-games* within the complex weave and rapid flow of life.

---

[1]Following convention, titles for Wittgenstein's works are abbreviated (PI = PhilosophicalInvestigations, RFM = Remarks on the Foundation of Mathematics, OC = On Certainty, WL = Wittgenstein's Lectures, CV = Culture Value, PO = Philosophical Occasions), with section (§) or page number (p.), with full citation and initials (e.g., RFM) in the References. See Abbreviation list, p. ii??

[2]Excerpt from Stickney (2005), *Philosophy of Education Society* paper. For a more detailed survey of how Wittgenstein has been taken up in Philosophy of Education, see Stickney and Peters 2017.



M. A. Peters and J. Stickney, *Wittgenstein's Education: 'A Picture Held Us Captive'*, SpringerBriefs on Key Thinkers in Education
https://doi.org/10.1007/978-981-10-8411-9_4

Attention to *mastery of techniques* shows how 'we' acquire embodied forms of practical reason: a stabilizing *habitus* of rule-following behaviours, norms and certainties. Contextual reading of the especially intriguing teaching cases, alongside Wittgenstein's anthropological cases and thought-experiments, points to how the pupil can also overcome this training. Gradually the pupil comes to operate within the norm, autonomous of the instructor's direction; the further possibility exists of coming to question some of the rules and fundamental *bedrock* deposited or absorbed in the training (OC §130; Z §310–34, 410–32). Together these cases show: (a) how training constitutes subjects in collective, normative ways of acting, *seeing-as* and judging (i.e. initiation into *forms of life* and *world-pictures*); and (b) the extent to which these shared forms of agreement and judgment are arbitrary and open to renegotiation (PI §241–2; Z §320). Approaching Wittgenstein's method in this way, we escape a conservative and gain a more liberal reading of agency in his later philosophy. The purpose of both sets is to help free us from deeply ingrained pictures that hold us captive (PI §115), and thus to undertake ethical work on transforming ourselves (PI, p. x; RFM §IV.53; CV 16e).

### 4.1.1 Two Profiles of Wittgenstein's Philosophical Method

Scenes of instruction give us a half-silhouette of Wittgenstein's later philosophy. Like a profile, we get from this picture one side of the persona Wittgenstein presented in the corpus. The other side of the face—the second profile he repeatedly gives us— are the thought-experiments, chimeras and encounters with aliens, which I will refer to as the 'anthropological cases'. Instead of opening a window onto pedagogic scenes, these latter passages transport us to distant lands where we see people but 'cannot find ourselves in them'—virtual others we 'can't find our feet with' (e.g., PI §223; RPII §30, 700).

In reading the learning cases we have to locate them, along with the anthropological, within Wittgenstein's more general statements on methodology. To gain a *synoptic view* of language-in-use and rule-following behaviour (going on *like this* and following 'blindly'), he says, we have to simplify a little. We need to limit what it is we are looking at within the *hurly-burly* (Z §567–69) and narrow our focus onto very clear, well-crafted and familiar cases: ones where the educated reader may instantly provide (recall) the appropriate background, and thus reduce the need for explicating minute details in the surroundings that contribute to sense. Telescoping into the teacher–learner situation provides this kind of clarity amid confusion, useful for explicating complex philosophical issues. Wittgenstein explains this as a way of looking at grammatical problems, 'of fundamental importance' to philosophy.

> A main source of our failure to understand is that we do not *command a clear* view of the use of our words. – Our grammar is lacking in this sort of perspicuity. A perspicuous representation produces just that understanding which consists in 'seeing connexions'. Hence the importance of finding and inventing *intermediate* cases. (PI §122)

The discovered and invented *intermediate cases* provide some interstice in the flow of life, pausing to show us grammatical traps at the foundation of knowledge, default positions in our thinking and category mistakes in the web of concepts that bind us. Throughout Wittgenstein's work, he is either finding cases of learning, likely drawn from his own teaching experience but intelligible to all readers 'bound together by science and education' (OC §171, 298) or he is fabricating them. The latter include illustratively absurd conditions where the 'general facts of nature' do not hold fast: cases where rulers stretch (RFM 1.5) and ink disappears (PI II, p. 226). Here 'things appear quite different from what they actually are': ...'rule becomes exception and exception rule'—cheese now grows and shrinks on the scale, making the practice of weighing to fix a price quite meaningless (PI §142). These foreign situations show us what is otherwise taken for granted, and therefore hidden from us because of its familiarity (PI §129). Both sets of *intermediate cases* are the medium of his later philosophy: through them, we come to see the foundations of language for acting and judging as we do. Medina (2002, 193) calls this a *deflationary* (not a quietist) approach to philosophical problems: one in which we dissolve them through inspection of everyday practices and their contravention. It is also a *decelerating* approach, in that it slows down our investigation by piling up examples, until it occurs to us that there is a faulty picture at work in the numerous cases presented. Collectively they show the *fly the way out of the fly-bottle* (PI §309–10).

At the outset of the *Investigations,* Wittgenstein says that pedagogic examples are provided to show what is otherwise obscured (see PI §§5–6 in Ch 1). Scenes of children learning language have an expository or heuristic purpose, showing inculcation into normative practices of usage. His argument in the *Investigations* and in *Philosophical Grammar* is that *ostensive teaching* (the pointing to link a word to a thing) remains ambiguous until *ostensive definition* provides broader, normative context of use (see Medina 2002, 169–70; cf. Ch 1).

> Let us imagine a rule intimating to me which way I am to obey it; that is, as my eye travels along the line, a voice within me says: '*This* way!' – What is the difference between this process of obeying a kind of inspiration and that of obeying a rule? For they are surely not the same. In the case of inspiration I *await* direction. I shall not be able to teach anyone else my 'technique' of following the line. Unless, indeed, I teach him some way of hearkening, some kind of receptivity. But then, of course, I cannot require him to follow the line in the same way as I do.
>
> These are not my experiences of acting from inspiration and according to a rule; they are grammatical notes. (PI §232)

Wittgenstein presents these models of usage for descriptive instead of prescriptive purposes: 'Our clear and simple language-games are not intended to be preparatory studies for a future regularization of language' (as though ignoring friction and air resistance, he adds). 'The language-games are rather set up as *objects of comparison* which are meant to throw light on the facts of our language by way not only of similarities, but also of dissimilarities' (PI §130). Such examples bring us '*back to the rough ground*' (PI §107), preventing philosophy from collapsing into vacuity or dogmatism (see Johansson 2017).

> For we can avoid ineptness or emptiness in our assertions only by presenting the model as what it is, as an object of comparison… (PI §131).

Practical and hypothetical cases prevent philosophy from becoming either prescriptive or idealistic.

> We want to establish an order in our knowledge of the use of language: an order with a particular end in view; one out of many possible orders; not *the* order. To this end we shall constantly be giving prominence to distinctions which our ordinary forms of language easily make us overlook. This may make it look as if we saw it as out task to reform language. (PI §132)

Perspicuous inspection of actual cases of language usage, or the drawing of distinctions by creating chimerical examples that throw language into greater relief, helps us to 'stop doing philosophy when we want to' (PI §133/Z §314). It is a pedagogical way of working on our selves. His approach—one form of therapy among many, not *the* method—is intended to alleviate the torment of certain problems that haunt philosophers by showing that these stem from deeply entrenched pictures in our language (PI §15, 133). Wittgenstein's examples show us how pictures are sedimented into the bedrock of our language through early training: our initiation into ways of thinking/acting/seeing.

### *4.1.2 Exemplification*

An application of this twofold approach comes across most clearly in his 'Lectures on Aesthetics' (c. 1938, in his Cambridge rooms) where he looks at how aesthetic words (another kind of conceptual 'tool') are used to describe 'good' or 'bad' art (see LC 1–2). Abandoning the theoretical approach for the descriptive one (see PI §§108–9), he asks us not imagine descriptions or attitudes that convey 'unheard of detail' (LC 35) or that demonstrate a 'craving for simplicity' in their explanatory method (LC 36).

> One thing we always do when discussing a word is to ask how we were taught it. Doing this on the one hand destroys a variety of misconceptions, on the other hand gives you a primitive language in which the word is used. Although this language is not what you talk when you are twenty, you get a rough approximation to what kind of language game is going to be played. Cf. How did we learn 'I dreamt so and so'? The interesting point is that we didn't learn it by being shown a dream. If you ask yourself how a child learns 'beautiful', 'fine', etc., you find it learns them roughly as interjections. …A child generally applies a word like 'good' first to food. One thing that is immensely important in teaching is exaggerated gestures and facial expressions. The word is taught as a substitute for a facial expression or gesture. The gestures, tones of voice, etc., in this case are expressions of approval. What *makes* the word an interjection of approval? It is the game it appears in, not the form of words. (LC 5–6)

He elaborates around the simple and yet rich example: 'That is a fine dress' (on well-tailored coats, see LC 5 and 13):

> In order to get clear about aesthetic words you have to describe a way of living. We have to talk about aesthetic judgements like 'That is beautiful', but we find that if we talk about aesthetic judgments we don't find these words at all, but a word used something like a gesture, accompanying a complicated activity. (LC 11)

Indicating what he means by a 'vast structure of activities' surrounding aesthetic judgments or expressions, he notes: 'What belongs to a language-game is a whole culture' (LC 9). We explored his deep contextualism in Chap. 2, also looking there at training in relation to aesthetics. Here we pause to note, in concluding *Wittgenstein's Education*, that he was not simply preoccupied with pupils learning how to carry out numerical series (PI §§141–242), but with the broader sense of a people's enculturation and cultivation (see Bowell 2017, on *bildung*). In this lecture he offers as examples, whether in a given society the children perform concerts, or whether the women also participate in the choirs as they do in Vienna (LC 8). How people react to the innovations of composers depends so much on their shared 'agreements of judgement' within a *form of life* (PI §§241–2), in which each composer has contributed to the accumulated and now crystallized 'rules' governing music over time (LC 6).[3] There is no scientific, behaviouristic or statistical way of capturing this kind of cultivation of aesthetic appreciation (LC 11, 21, 33). These higher forms of participation and response point us in the direction of what is ineffable, and although technically 'senseless' (on *Tractarian* ground, see Ch 1)—ultimately the most meaningful aspects of life.

After considering the pedagogic cases, he then entertains an invented one:

> If you came to a foreign tribe, whose language you didn't know at all and wished to know what words corresponded to 'good', 'fine', etc., what would you look for? You would look for smiles, gestures, food, toys. (LC 6)

Wittgenstein imagines spherical 'people' on Mars with sticks coming out of their bodies: alien life forms that could not gesture to us. In such an unfamiliar place, we would not know what to look for (LA §6), and we would feel as though we could not *understand* such strange beings (Z §390). In Z §383, for instance he imagines a tribe where such severe training has occurred, people do not respond to pain stimulus as we do: never speaking of feelings pain or using interjections to express hurt. Not sharing in their extreme regime of training, we could not 'find our feet' with such people (Z §390). Each of these intermediate cases or grammatical investigations point back to our *form of life* as the basis for judging meaningful speech, gesture and action; this observation, of forms of life as our ground for judging (PI §§241–2), in turn, presupposes initiate training into customary patterns or techniques of 'going-on as others do', taking us back to Wittgenstein's patient

[3]You can say that every composer changed the rules but the variation was very slight; not all the rules were changed. The music was still very good by a great many of the old rules. (LC 6)

build up to this point through many scenes of instruction, including the rule-following series from PI §§140–242.

> ...What is the criterion for the way the formula is meant? Presumably the way we always use it, the way we were taught to use it. (RFM 1.1–2)

The philosophical concern here is not how we should train children, but why it appears to be arbitrary how they respond to the rules being taught, and how our only criterion of judgement as to whether they are performing or understand correctly is their ability to react appropriately to the training given.

> Following a rule is analogous to obeying an order. We are trained to do so; we react to an order in a particular way. But what if one person reacts in one way and another in another to the order and training? Which one is right?
>
> Suppose you came as an explorer into an unknown country with a language quite strange to you. In what circumstances would you say that the people there gave ordered, understood them, obeyed them, rebelled against them, and so on?
>
> The common behaviour of mankind is the system of reference by means of which we interpret an unknown language. (PI §206)

In PI §207, he creates a thought-experiment about these same people from a strange land, but adds that although they *apparently* speak an articulate language, when we try to learn their language 'we find it impossible to do so. For there is no regular connexion between what they say, the sounds they make, and their actions'. In this extreme case, where action is disconnected from sounds, 'There is not enough regularity for us to call it "language"' (PI 207).

It should now be obvious that Wittgenstein is not commenting on how to instruct pupils in carrying out numerical sequences, even though he may have been drawing on his own experience in teaching young children in developing these illustrative cases. The philosophical purpose is to show that, contrary to what rationalists would suggest, pupils do not have to have the rules clearly formulated in their heads in order to carry on as expected by the instructor, and should a pupil deviate from the intended rule there is only the agreement of the masters or adepts to serve as a basis for clarification. The same can be said for having been trained into comprehension of the ostensive definitions of words; once acquired, we do not need to be able to articulate the grammatical rules that govern their usage.

> ...not only do we not think of the rules of usage – of definitions, etc. – while using language, but when we are asked to give such rules, in most cases we aren't able to do so. We are unable clearly to circumscribe the concepts we use; not because we don't know their real definition, but because there is no real 'definition' to them. (BB 25)

Faced with what Wittgenstein describes as an infinite regress problem, where every attempt to interpret the rule begs another explanation or justification, he has only our training into practices or our mastery of techniques as the final ground of judgment.

> If I have exhausted the justifications I have reached bedrock, and my spade is turned. Then I am inclined to say: "This is simply what I do." (PI §217)

Unable to dig further, he turns instead of our *form of life* as a way of depicting this fluid or living 'ground', fully aware that this could be read as taking us down a path toward relativism where 'truth' means adherence to custom or tradition instead of verification through empirical means (see Ch 2, re: *forms of life*, RPP I §630; see PI, p. 226; PI §§241–2). Aware that this grounding in *forms of life* could be read as relativism, he ends the rule-following sequence by conceding that there is no external authority for ascertaining whether the pupil adheres to the rule correctly (the paradox as set out in PI §206). In the absence of externally verifiable grounds, he can only show how we were taught or trained to hold certain propositions *as* 'true', or affirm judgments as 'correct'.

> Asking whether and how a proposition can be verified is only a particular way of asking "How d'you mean?" The answer is a contribution to the grammar of the proposition. (PI §353)
>
> Our knowledge forms an enormous system. And only within this system has a particular bit the value we give it. (PI §410).
>
> [Not that I could describe the system of these convictions. Yet my convictions do form a system, a structure.] (OC §102)
>
> All testing, all confirmation and disconfirmation of a hypothesis takes place already within a system. And this system is not a more or less arbitrary and doubtful point of departure for all our arguments: no, it belongs to the essence of what we call an argument. The system is not so much the point of departure, as the element in which arguments have their life. (OC §105)
>
> We do not learn the practice of making empirical judgments by learning rules: we are taught *judgments* and their connexion with other judgments. A *totality* of judgments is made plausible to us. (OC §140)
>
> When we first begin to believe anything, what we believe is not a single proposition, it is a whole system of propositions. (Light dawns gradually over the whole.) (OC §141)
>
> There are countless general empirical propositions that count as certain for us. (OC §273)
>
> I am taught that under *such* circumstances *this* happens. It has been discovered by making the experiment a few times. Not that that would prove anything to us, if it weren't that this experience was surrounded by others which combine with it to form a system. Thus, people did not make experiments just about falling bodies but also about air resistance and all sorts of things.
>
> But in the end I rely on these experiences, or on the reports of them, I feel no scruples about ordering my own activities in accordance with them. – But hasn't this trust proven itself? So far as I can judge – yes. (OC §603)

Pointing to our initiation into *forms of life* as the ground of judgment (PI §§241–2) sets limit-conditions on our knowledge and our ability to give reasons or justifications for why we act or believe the way we do (see Ch 2). But this move is not intended to trivialize or take for granted the processes of developing and transmitting knowledge, as he is not abandoning his own education in engineering or engaging in scepticism about the veracity of our various domains of knowledge.

> Whether the earlier experience is the cause of the certainty depends on the system of hypotheses, or natural laws, in which we are considering the phenomenon of certainty.

> Is our confidence justified? – What people accept as justification – is shewn by how they think and live. (PI §325; cf. PI, p. 200)

Nor is Wittgenstein acquiescing to forms of indoctrination, as though it does not matter what we are trained to think.

> The effect of making men think in accordance with dogmas,.... It is not a wall setting limits to what can be believed, but more like a brake which, however, practically serves the same purpose; it's almost as though someone were to attach a weight to your foot to restrict your freedom of movement. (CV 28e)

We cannot get outside our residency within *language-games,* into which we have become habituated through training, but we can assess their relative degrees of certainty.

> I can be as *certain* of someone else's sensations as of any fact. But this does not make the propositions "He is depressed", and "25 × 25 = 625" and "I am sixty years old" into similar instruments. The explanation suggests itself that the certainty is of a different *kind.* – This seems to point to a psychological difference. But the difference is logical. ... 'Mathematical certainty' is not a psychological concept.
>
> The kind of certainty is the kind of language-game. (PI, p. 224)

Within the broader context of *forms of life*, Wittgenstein reveals how training into our second nature leads to spontaneous, customary reactions that do not require prior thought or interpretation (PI §198): either in their performance by the pupil or in the judgment of their propriety by the instructor (see Ch 2).

Learning how to operate within *language-games* is something belonging to our 'natural history', as he puts it (PI §25), and reliant on our natural reactions within a shared form of life, onto which *language-games* are grafted. Dogs cannot engage in what we know as 'hope' because they have not mastered the *language-games* of hoping in our *form of life* (PI, p. 174, 229), nor could we understand lions even if they could talk (PI, p. 223). 'By nature and by particular training, a particular education, we are disposed to give spontaneous expression to wishes in certain circumstances' (PI §441). In Z §545 he asks us to consider how a child learns the use of the word 'pain', as a kind of associative behaviour. The attempt at explaining the learning process results in a dead end.

> *What* does this explanation explain? Ask yourself – *What* sort of ignorance does it remove? – Being sure that someone is in pain, doubting whether he is, and so on, are so many natural, instinctive, kinds of behaviour towards other human beings, and our language is merely an extension of this relation. Our *language-game* is an extension of primitive behaviour. (For our language-game is behaviour.) (Instinct) [4]

Putting cultivated, second-nature reactions at the core of our linguistic, mathematical and cultural behaviour is what Wittgenstein alluded to with his references to *forms of life*.

---

[4]See Z §540, 541, re: primitive reactions and prelinguistic behaviour on which we base the language-game of recognizing another's pain. (Cf. PI, p. 218: "What is the primitive reaction with which the language-game begins – which can then be translated into these words?")

> The primitive form of the language-game is certainty, not uncertainty. For uncertainty could never lead to action. I want to say: it is characteristic of our language that the foundation on which it grows consists of steady ways of living (*feste Lebensformen*), regular ways of acting. (PO 420)

> Our mistake is to look for an explanation where we ought to look at what happens as a "proto-phenomenon." That is, where we ought to have said: *this language-game is played.* (PI §654)

> Giving grounds, however, justifying the evidence, comes to an end; – but the end is not certain propositions' striking us immediately as true, i.e., it is not a kind of *seeing* on our part; it is our *acting*, which lies at the bottom of the language-game. (OC §204)[5]

> ...The primitive language-game taught to children needs no justification; attempts at justification need to be rejected. (PI, p. 200)

> Well, if everything speaks for an hypothesis and nothing against it – is it then certainly true? One may designate it as such. – But does it certainly agree with reality, with the facts? With this question you are already going around in a circle.

> To be sure there is justification; but justification comes to an end. (OC §§191–92)

## 4.2 Judging Teachers[6]

### *4.2.1 Analytic and Criterial Delineations of 'Teaching'*

During the 1970s, at the zenith of the analytic movement in philosophy of education, Hirst (1971) asked the deceptively simple question: How, upon entering a classroom, does the external inspector *know* that teaching is in fact taking place? Concerned during the 'experimental sixties' that some pedagogic techniques were merely parading as 'innovative teaching', Hirst and other analytic philosophers answered by sharpening the 'teaching' concept: the *necessary and sufficient conditions* for 'teaching' (qua teaching). Concept mapping of this sort was to give us clearer boundaries for such educational terms as 'teaching', seen as being an intentional, rational activity that is 'parasitic' upon the concept of 'learning' (see Peters and Stickney 2018). Reading Wittgenstein's case against private language to six-graders, Hirst argued (1971, 5), is not teaching, as it has no hope of uptake with the intended audience. Clarifying the 'teaching' concept would supposedly prevent educators from doing 'crazy and fuzzy things in its name'.

Category-rating systems developed in the 1970s offered checklists for inspectors to record whether students were engaged in suitable learning activities. Not just any method of obtaining 'learning' is justifiable; from a liberal-analytic view, 'teaching' as a rational activity is distinguished from 'conditioning' and 'training', and counterfeits of 'teaching' like 'proselytizing', 'advertising' or 'indoctrinating' (see

[5]Through training: "Our way of seeing is remodelled" (RFM IV.30).

[6]Excerpt from Stickney (2009).

Komisar 1968). Green (1968, 33) allowed fuzzy boundaries between these concepts bearing a 'family resemblance', heeding Wittgenstein's advice not to look for more clarity than exits within practice.

> ...not only do we not think of the rules of usage – of definitions, etc. – while using language, but when we are asked to give such rules, in most cases we aren't able to do so. We are unable clearly to circumscribe the concepts we use; not because we don't know their real definition, but because there is no real 'definition' to them. (BB 25)

Hirst and Peters (1970, 6, 133), on the other hand, looked for underlying criteria that would unify discrete sets. The fear among these analytic philosophers was that Wittgenstein's non-essentialism leads to either scepticism (inability to discern) or quietism (inability to articulate and stipulate differences; see Kripke 1982). Giving up on criteria or explicit rules suggests that we cannot rationally determine best candidates for 'teaching'. Public criteria instruct participants in how best to direct their efforts and appear to tighten practices of judging that might otherwise loosen into subjectivism, in which case 'anything goes'.

Paradoxically, escaping enthrallment in the overblown criteriological approach offers no escape (entirely) from criteria themselves; rather, complex practices, like repertoires of teaching acts or cases of professional development, become the criterion for recognizing something as *this* or *that.* Instead of the analytic project of searching for explicit criteria and rules for 'sound' teaching, we turn next to Wittgenstein's 'background' approach to *seeing* tacit criteria at work within living education practices (see Peters et al. 2008). From Wittgenstein's perspective, recognizing 'sound' or 'unsound' teaching practice requires initiate training and mastery of techniques, upon which practitioners learn to *see* something *as* criteria for something else.[7] In the final sections, we examine the political ramifications of this contextualist approach and offer demonstrations of its applications in educational settings. Without dismissing the criteriological approach, we question its tendency to conserve even arbitrary boundaries for practice. We may see in the earlier attempt to define 'teaching', coupled with modernist programs to standardize education, reactionary tendencies of the time that discourage fruitful experimentation and diminish eclecticism within the field.

### 4.2.2 *Wittgenstein's Background-Contextualism*

Wittgenstein's *Investigations* remind us that we need not explicitly interpret or hold a rule in our head in order to act in agreement, whether in playing chess or speaking. 'When I obey a rule, I do not choose. I obey the rule *blindly*' (PI §219).

[7]See Cavell (1979). Referring to gradual induction into a way of seeing and judging, as opposed to politically motivated interventions that redirect teachers onto mandated reforms. Emblematic of the latter, a York Region District School Board flyer in Ontario once advertised a workshop, run by consultants, to delineate 'sound' from 'unsound' teaching.

His deceivingly 'simple' cases of teaching students how to follow a mathematical rule demonstrates the problem in trying to specify each aspect of 'sound' teaching: efforts to justify or give reasons behind rule-following behaviour results in an infinite regress, where one interpretation chases after another and all hang in the air (PI §141, 198). Instead, 'no course of action could be determined by the rule, because every course of action can be made out to accord with the rule' (PI §201).

Pointing towards the 'groundlessness' and sometimes the arbitrariness of knowledge on the grander scale, he challenges us to accept an impermanent and shifting ground for our certainties, instead of seeking deeper forms of verification (OC §§63, 166, 248, 253). In his critique of epistemology, the complex weave of practices and reactions that constitute our *form of life* ultimately grounds our 'agreement in judgments', here concerning teachers, their pedagogic knowledge and the 'sanity' of their practices.[8] Wittgenstein's non-foundational argument takes us to the ultimate recognition of bedrock certainties and hinge propositions upon which we act and judge, unhesitatingly or unreflectively, within our given *form of life* (OC §§94–99, 141, 166, 248, 253; PI §410). He appeals to *forms of life* as 'the given' (PI §630; cf. PI, p. 226), the ungrounded terrain at which our spade is turned in searching for justifications (PI §217).

These *forms of life* are a hybrid of the animal reactions humans have in common and the second natures we continuously improvize through the myriad language-games we graft (without necessity or compulsion) onto these primitive ones (see Ch 2; cf. PI §§241–2 below).[9] This may give appearances of epistemic relativism, but it points instead to how we actually perform and react to signs within a community of language users.

> Consider how we learn to judge whether someone is colour blind, use the multiplication table to arrive at agreed answers, and weigh imponderable evidence in judging motives, intentions or emotions. We do these with considerable agreement, though with varying degrees of certainty.
>
> Is there such a thing as 'expert judgment' about the genuineness of expressions of feelings? – Even here, there are those whose judgment is 'better' and those whose judgment is 'worse'.

[8]Reading 'agreement in judgements' (PI §242) as referring to a consensus of action (not merely opinion; cf. RFM VII.39) among communities of practitioners, and not to what one might construe as a 'private practice'. The nagging question of private versus shared interpretations of rules (the old Baker & Hacker versus Malcolm debate) centres on PI §199, where Wittgenstein ponders whether a practice could be performed only once (possibly by a single practitioner). Wittgenstein appears to answer his interlocutor definitively in terms of shared customs or institutions of usage (cf. PI §23) into which we are trained to react in a particular, customary manner (cf. PI §198), thus giving a 'regular' instead of am idiosyncratic use to such things as sign-posts or pointing gestures. In PI §201 he clarifies further that obeying a rule is a practice, and that unlike merely thinking the rule there is no possibility of private practice of the rule (cf. §206, where he further sets the training and 'common behaviour of mankind' as the necessary background for judging proper obeisance of rules).

[9]Re: Background and ineluctable neurological capacities see Searle (1995), 146–7.

> Corrector prognoses will generally issue from the judgments of those with better knowledge of mankind.
>
> Can one learn this knowledge? Yes; some can. Not, however, by taking a course in it, but through "experience". Can someone else be a man's teacher in this? Certainly. From time to time he gives him the right tip. – That is what 'learning' and 'teaching' are like here. – What one acquires here is not a technique; one learns correct judgments. There are also rules, but they do not form a system, and only experienced people can apply them right. Unlike calculating rules.
>
> What is most difficult here is to put this indefiniteness, correctly and unfalsified, into words. (PI, p. 227)

Stating that those with "better knowledge of mankind" are more likely to succeed in mastering the practice of judging emotions, Wittgenstein points to how learning language-games of judging depends on the pupil's ability to make pertinent connections between this practice and the many others to which it is inextricably linked.

Reading pretence on someone's face—for instance, a child hoping to stay home from school or a teacher pretending to be enthusiastic in implementing reforms—requires almost instant reaction to subtle expressions that signal feigning, and instant value judgments as to a person's motives or character (see Kern 2004, on telling when a child is lying about being ill in order to stay home from school). 'Pretence', for Wittgenstein, is a *language-game* children learn to play, and adults learn to read more discerningly.

> A child must have developed far before it can pretend, must have learned a lot before it can simulate. (LW 42e; Cf. PI p. 229)

These kinds of judgments—seeing 'pretence', 'honesty' in the face—are 'surrounded by far-reaching manifestations of life' (PI §534; see Ch 2 re: background for judging actions, RPP 1 and 2, §624–26, 629).

It is difficult to put into words the background against which we judge individual human actions; its 'indefiniteness' leads us to speak in metaphorical terms (Z §569). Digging for a deeper foundation, other than this complex 'web' of interrelated practices, is often fruitless; consequently, Wittgenstein would have us stop at the level of our culturally ingrained and natural ways of reacting (Z §540, 541, 545; PI, p. 218). Attempts to articulate this complex background—what makes our signs and gestures intelligible—simply relies upon further background; full explication, like complete disengagement, is, therefore, impossible, thus undermining the traditional goal of epistemology as a foundational philosophy (see Taylor 1995, 11).

The danger of resurrecting criteria is that we easily fall into a picture of 'thinking as an incorporeal process', rather like the Devil separating Schlemiehl's shadow from the ground (PI §339). As José Medina explains, for Wittgenstein what matters is not manifesting the criterion of identity in which we are already conversant (PI §253), as much as learning to see exemplars as demonstrative guides to practice.

> This suggests an immanent perspective according to which there are no criteria of identity and correctness outside (or in abstraction from) our actual practices. The only criterion of identity is what as a matter of contingent fact counts as the same in practice. There is no

> criterial authority for what counts as the same beyond what is actually taken as such by rule followers, beyond what they do in repeated performance. (Medina 2006, 28–29)

What Wittgenstein shows is that the rules or criteria do not exist outside the practice of judging, though we might reconstruct them after the fact (PI §90). Teachers cannot convey them except through a process of initiation into the practice and mastery of making such judgments, but the lack of articulated criteria or plan does not make the judgment any less certain (cf. Z §§570, 575–6).

> How does someone who accepts a criterion as certain differ from someone who doesn't? (LW, p. 87e)

> But does accepting no criterion as certain mean: never being certain that someone else feels this way or that? Can I be not quite certain and yet accept no criterion as certain? I am (behave) certain, but for instance I don't know *why*. (LW, p. 87e)

How do you know, for instance when someone correctly uses the word 'think'? Wittgenstein reminds us that we know and recognize correct applications even though we cannot describe the complex circumstances that underlie normal usage.

> One learns the word 'think', i.e., its use, under certain circumstances, which, however, one does not learn to describe. (Z §114)

> But I *can teach* a person the use of the word! For a description of the circumstances is not needed for that. (Z §115; cf. OC§§ 545–8)

### 4.2.3 Exemplification: Retelling in the Classroom

Imagine the familiar language-game of a pupil asking the teacher for clarification, taking place under the purview of an inspector. Under 'normal' circumstances, the student and the external observer would appraise the quality of the teacher's re-explanation based on whether it satisfactorily gave the student a new angle of approach from which to apprehend the matter or merely repeated the previous explanation. Subtleties of tone and gesture matter greatly, as the teacher's performance of re-explaining may invite the student to re-enter the problem space from a new angle. Alternately, stress in the voice and rigidity in the body may signal disapproval: insinuating that the first explanation was sufficient for an attentive, 'good' student.

John Hunter points out that in such teaching circumstances, subjects do not rely on external criteria to judge the suitability of retelling; it will be a localized matter of agreement in judgment, the rules for which are contained in the shared language-games of classroom telling and retelling (see Hunter 1973, 1985). The student and inspector react to the teacher's re-explanation, with approval or disapproval, without the analytic ratiocination that Hirst would have us apply. There is no interpretive act in this case; Wittgenstein refers to this as 'a way of grasping a rule that is not an interpretation' (PI §201): 'When I follow a sign-post, the connection between it and my action is not mediated by an interpretation of sign-posts that I acquired when I was trained in their use. I simply act as I have been trained'.[10]

In the teaching situation, or in the flow of classroom practice, there is potential room to negotiate ranges of reasonableness or tolerance, without turning to outside criteria to serve as a guide. We can list some evaluative criteria for form and content, such as 'articulation is clear' instead of cajoling and 'goes beyond mere repetition'. Erecting such criteria, however, may give the false impression that we are interpreting the teaching phenomena under observation (retelling) according to fixed criteria, whereas Wittgenstein calls attention to a form of *seeing*—instantaneous recognition of signs.

## 4.3 Teacher Autonomy Within Curricular Rules[11]

Wittgenstein's remarks on rule-following and training offer philosophical lenses on a significant finding of the study into teaching and learning philosophy in Ontario high schools[12]: the myriad ways teachers enact curricular mandates in the Ministry's curriculum. Starting with prescriptive, normative rules (thou shalt), how do school systems end up with archipelagos of diverse interpretation instead of the curricular-alignment envisioned by policymakers? Instead of rules being determinant,[13] Wittgenstein notes, in enacting them we end up with multiple interpretations possibly in accordance, and thus 'any interpretation hangs in the air with what it interprets' (PI §198). Carrying out numerical sequences, for instance rules do not compel us to follow the intended series.

> 'But am I not compelled, then, to go the way I do in a chain of inference?' Compelled? After all, I can presumably go as I choose! 'But if you want to remain in accord with the rules you must go this way'. Not at all, I call this 'accord'. 'Then you have changed the meaning of the word 'accord', or the meaning of the rule'. No; – who says what 'change' and 'remaining the same' mean here? (RFM I.113)

Wittgenstein concludes that this ambiguity threatens to undermine our concept of rule-deviation.

> This was our paradox: no course of action could be determined by a rule, because every course of action can be made out to accord with the rule. … if everything can be made out to accord with the rule, then it can also be made out to conflict with it. (PI §201)

---

[10]See McDowell (1998, 239) on education, *Bildung* and enculturation into second natures. Bowell (2017) discusses *Bildung* in relation to Wittgenstein.

[11]Stickney's Excerpt from a Symposium on High School Philosophy Teaching, with Trevor Norris and Lauren Bialytstok, *Philosophy of Education Society of Great Britain* (Oxford 2017; Session Chair, Michael Hand).

[12]Dr. Trevor Norris, Brock University: Principal Investigator, Social Science and Humanities Research Grant, *High School Philosophy Project* (Ontario, Canada). https://hsphil.weebly.com/. (Stickney was a co-investigator in the project.)

[13]Rules, for instance, do not prescribe how high to throw the tennis ball when serving (PI §68–70).

Ambivalence leads to critical realization: misunderstanding stems from the expectation of intended rules having authority, whereas instead we find an infinite regress where alternate plausible interpretations loom behind one another, making them more like different 'expressions of the rule' (PI §201). As in responding to sign-posts: proceeding is less deliberative or reasoned-through, more second-nature ways of reacting instantaneously to directives (cf. PI §198; cf. Z §355).

> ...What this shews is that there is a way of grasping a rule which is not an interpretation, but which is exhibited in what we call "obeying the rule" and "going against it" in actual cases. (PI §201; cf. RFM I.113)

'Teachers may interpret rules' for their students by means of training, but this understanding of how to go on or react accordingly presupposes internalization of tacit knowledge and practices absorbed previously through one's cultural surroundings (RFM VII.47; cf. Burbules 2008). Different regimes of training, reactions, or circumstances lead to some 'obeying' or 'going against' intended rules.

A brief synopsis of Ontario's Grade 12 Philosophy curriculum illustrates what accord/discord means in this context. The Ministry prescribes coverage of at least two of the three core units: metaphysics, ethics and epistemology. Additionally, teachers must address philosophical reasoning (including logic) and research skills, and include one of three optional units: philosophy of science, political philosophy and/or aesthetics. For an introductory survey of philosophy, this structure allows some flexibility, letting teachers weigh the opportunity costs of breadth versus specialization. Units are then broken down into overall and specific curricular expectations such as 'covering philosophical terminology' or 'addressing schools of thought', creating a filamentary structure that tightens down what units should convey in content and skills. Additionally, the curriculum 'prompts' teachers as to which thinkers might be used, but these are merely exemplars/guide-posts.

A teacher interviewed in the *High School Philosophy Project* study ('Mr. Aristotle') noted that teachers would be advised to adhere to these curricular 'laws', but in most cases, noncompliant teachers are not held to account: even during periodic but infrequent inspections. If logic or philosophy of science appeared on the course outline/syllabus but were not in fact taught (or expectations sufficiently met in the effort), as often happens due to either complexity or time constraints, it is unlikely these lapses would be noticed. In Wittgenstein's scenes-of-instruction, rule compliance is secured through strict regimes of training, uptake of which results in obeying rules blindly (PI §219). Philosophy teachers are unlikely to have had strict or formal training in the Ministry curriculum, glossed over even within educational institutes. Instead of authorities cajoling teachers into heeding rules, in most cases teachers work alone or in small teams, negotiating curriculum primarily with students and possibly a colleague or department head. Isolation and autonomy leads to divergent evolution in how the philosophy curriculum is interpreted or enacted. Provincial subject-associations (Ontario Philosophy Teachers Association) offer exposure to educators working outside their school, broadening horizons (genealogically speaking) in terms of how philosophy could be taught otherwise.

Newer teachers may be less improvisatory, as two decades of tacit training in expectations-based curricula have instilled a 'paint-by-numbers' approach to curriculum design: practices reinforcing inclinations to stay 'on colour' and 'within lines'. Textbook editors, of course, faithfully adhere to Ministry structure and heed prompts in order to gain provincial approval, making text-usage a subtle form of compliance training. Hard, say, to use the Ministry-congruent McGraw-Hill textbook without blindly following sanctioned orders or 'rule-expressions'. But historians may react differently, assembling topics not as discrete units (metaphysics, then ethics) but scattered diachronically as they appear in the Classical, Enlightenment or Modern periods, arranging themes in a way that goes against the curriculum writer's intention of avoiding a history-of-ideas type organization. Teachers with less philosophy training may draw on their social science education to create issue-oriented courses (as prescribed in the Grade 11 curriculum), pulling in some aspects of core and optional units as they appear relevant, both topically and within the aperture of the teacher's grasp. Some, like Stickney (see 2014), push the limits in trying to teach Wittgenstein to secondary students (also in Stickney et al. 2011, Ch 11). Hazardously, some stray completely from the curriculum, making courses idiosyncratic. Remarkably, Ontario's *International Baccalaureate* teachers offer 'Theory of Knowledge' (supposedly not 'epistemology') either as 'Philosophy' (public) or 'Religious Studies' (Catholic), playing with three conflicting sets of rules: different games. At a certain point, we might say, these teachers are not necessarily 'wrong' but are no longer playing the same language-games of 'philosophy' (unlike cooking, 'if you follow other rules than those of chess you are playing another game'; see Z §320 in Ch 3; cf., PI §§496–499).

The view we are conveying and defending is one the of considerable but delicate teacher agencies: what Tully (2002/2003, after Wittgenstein and Foucault) refers to as 'civic freedoms within the rules'. Cautionary notes on rule-entanglement (PI §125; see Ch 3): Although curriculum is mostly created and delivered out of administrative purview, the cumulative effect of neoliberal accountability reforms has been increasing to open this scene of educational freedom to inspection and intrusive control. Defence comes from teachers' most significant, prior training in university Philosophy courses. More 'circumstantially', though, teachers react to educational mandates based on the broader academic *ethos* of their liberal education: internalized background or bedrock (OC §§94–98) for their current 'agreements in judgment' (PI §242) when designing curricula—including the aims of education and axiological schema governing how philosophy customarily fits into secondary education in our *form of life*.

## 4.4 Conclusion: 'A Picture Holds Us Captive'

> Grammar tells us what kind of object anything is. (PI §373)
>
> Words have meaning only in the stream of life. (LW I §913; cf. Z §173–4)

In the *Philosophical Investigations* Wittgenstein (1953) writes:

> A picture held us captive. And we could not get outside it, for it lay in our language and language seemed to repeat it to us inexorably.—When philosophers use a word —"knowledge", "being", "object", "I", "proposition", "name"— and try to grasp the essence of the thing, one must always ask oneself: is the word ever actually used in this way in the language-game which is its original home?—What we do is to bring words back from their metaphysical to their everyday use. (PI §115)

The notion of 'picture' here and corresponding notions of 'worldview' and 'world picture' that Wittgenstein uses in *On Certainty* as part of his disassembly of Cartesian epistemology fundamentally shifts the concept of philosophy and its practice away from arguments and the force of argumentation to the context of 'worldview' or *Weltanschuung,* as a deeply embedded cultural paradigm or cognitive orientation, and the question of how one changes a worldview. The concept in English is a troubled concept with a troubled history.

In the German tradition, the concept *Weltanschuung* has a rich and complex history that strongly influenced Wittgenstein. *Weltanschuung* was used first by Kant and later popularized by Hegel. It was given a linguistic reading in Humboldt's key concept of *Weltansicht* (world sight or attitude). Often the term in the German tradition is given an organic reading that emphasized syntactic and meaning structures that characterise a people, a language and territory, and also, by implication, a set of fundamental values and beliefs. Sometimes the organic reading is supported through the folk tradition of music and literature that has grown up in a culture that come to express an organic unity. Often in the past, the concept also expresses a fundamental belief orientation of a lived religion that deals with basic questions of life and the afterlife. Philosophically, *Weltanschuung* was bought into the discussion in the nineteenth and twentieth centuries as a result of increasing contact between cultures and especially in relation to questions of cultural and linguistic relativity, rationalism and universality. One guiding theme that animated discussion was how do worldviews grow and develop both historically and organically. Another question is how to, analyze, change and assess them. In what sense can they be articulated, understood, compared and developed?

In their work *Worldviews: From Fragmentation to Integration* Aerts et al. (2007, 13) identify seven components of a worldview on the basis of seven questions:

1. What is the nature of our world? How is it structured and how does it function?
2. Why is our world the way it is, and not different? Why are we the way we are, and not different? What kind of global explanatory principles can we put forward?
3. Why do we feel the way we feel in this world, and how do we assess global reality, and the role of our species in it?
4. How are we to act and to create in this world? How, in what different ways, can we influence the world and transform it? What are the general principles by which we should organize our actions?
5. What future is open to us and our species in this world? By what criteria are we to select these possible futures?
6. How are we to construct our image of this world in such a way that we can come up with answers to (1), (2) and (3)?
7. What are some of the partial answers that we can propose to these questions?

In constructing modern worldviews the authors 'situate ourselves in the difficult but necessary tension between Modernism and Post modernism, Scientism and Anthropocentrism, Enlightenment and Romanticism, secularism and religion, philosophy and science, the individual and the collective, western and non-western culture' (p. 12). It is clear that the discussion of worldview is a German problematic (problem set) that uniquely defines the question of globalization. It is also a problematic that becomes increasingly significant in the work of Wittgenstein not only to understand philosophical problems that take the form of emerging, changing and seemingly conflicting *Weltanschuung*, as involving the assessment of a cultural ensemble or totality, but also historical shifts in philosophical worldviews such as that between Cartesianism and *what comes after*; what comes after … essences? the cogito? body/mind dualism? modernism in philosophy? foundationalism? and so on.

The central notion of 'pictures' (see Ch 1) demonstrates how Wittgenstein was historically sensitized to the German tradition of *Weltanschuung* and how it comes to represent something characteristic of Wittgenstein's style of philosophy and the kind of problems that he tried to address. We are concerned to show how both of these philosophical concerns impact on pedagogy: how do we escape the 'picture that holds us captive'? Certainly, not solely by advancing arguments. How do people substitute one worldview for another? And pedagogically speaking, how should we proceed then?

### 4.4.1 'A Picture Held Us Captive' in the *Investigations*

In the immediate context of the *Investigations,* Wittgenstein seems to be referring to the ideas that he put forward in the *Tractatus* and specifically the question of pictorial form of the proposition: '…the general form of a proposition is: This is how things are'. There are a number of things that we can note about this passage.

First, it seems to involve a repudiation of earlier views especially the notion that propositions picture the world, that is facts, by virtue of its logical structure. The proposition thus displays its logical form through a kind of isomorphism. We might generalize to say that the early Wittgenstein suggests that the logical form of the proposition that shows itself is a mirror in the syntax of the language. Here are examples drawn from his early *Tractatus*:

> The fact that the elements of a picture are related to one another in a determinate way represents that things are related to one another in the same way. Let us call this connexion of its elements the structure of the picture, and let us call the possibility of this structure the pictorial form of the picture. (TLP §2.15)
>
> Pictorial form is the possibility that things are related to one another in the same way as the elements of the picture. That is how a picture is attached to reality; it reaches right out to it. (TLP §9 2.151–2.1511)
>
> 'The facts in logical space are the world ... Each thing is, as it were, in a space of possible states of affairs. This space I can imagine empty, but I cannot imagine the thing without the space (TLP 3 1.13, 4 2.013).
>
> 'The totality of true propositions is the whole of natural science (or the whole corpus of the natural sciences' (TLP 4.1 l), and if 'Logic pervades the world: the limits of the world are also its limits' (TLP 3 5.61)

Second, what is significant is this investigation is a linguistic one and not an epistemological one. Fact-stating language is able to picture facts by mirroring a logical structure that exists in the world. Understanding the logic of language, therefore, is the basis for determining which language forms lead us astray. Language provides the 'deep grammar' for our worldview and contains within it a metaphysics of subject and object that determines the notion of self and its relation to reality. Third, the aim of philosophy is to question these basic distinctions and to transcend the culture from within by engaging in a 'battle against the bewitchment of or intelligence by means of language' (PI §109) with the aim of showing 'the fly the way out of the fly-bottle' (PI §309). Fourth and more broadly, Wittgenstein's remarks at (§115) can be construed as an attack on the Cartesian worldview, a demonstration of the problems associated with this kind of thinking and the metaphysics of essences. Cartesianism as the form of philosophical modernity cannot be dismissed on the basis of argument—it is not open to argument—what is required is something much more fundamental that employs an approach to language that can work on us like a therapy to focus on everyday use of words in their language-game and release us from the temptation to use words philosophically, removed from the context of their use.

The truly revolutionary aspect of Wittgenstein's thinking is that he did not want to offer an alternative or another metaphysical system to replace the Cartesian worldview. His aim was to liberate human beings from the metaphysical picture that held us captive, a captivity based on pictures or deep metaphors, that views modern philosophy as having firm foundations and essences where knowledge is based on accurate representations of the world. As Naugle (2002) argues, Wittgenstein wants to replace the Cartesian worldview with the non-Cartesian worldview (*Weltbild*) that rests on unverifiable *forms of life* that recognizes non-representational functions of language. Naugle (2002, 148) suggests:

> In attempting to change the human way of seeing, Wittgenstein introduces a new epoch into Western thinking. Whereas Plato upheld ontology and Descartes submitted epistemology as the primary concern, Wittgenstein nominated grammar and language as the governing principles. Major paradigm shifts in Western philosophy have run roughly from the Platonic form-world of being to the Cartesian inner world of knowledge to the Wittgenstein sayable-world of meaning.

Wittgenstein indicates that changing a worldview is not like changing one's mind and it doesn't happen easily because it is not an entirely rational process. Worldview core beliefs are held on to even in the face of evidence. Argument, even sustained argument, may have little effect on its own. This problem is really a *pedagogical* problem that involves a process of reviewing framework beliefs and facts, recognizing the system of beliefs and how they constitute a loose network of beliefs. No one fact or even orchestration of facts will necessarily move people to change their views partly because they are so deeply embedded that it does not occur to believers that the worldview is even able to be challenged. It is akin to the same philosophical space as changing one's mind but much more complex. We can learn from the discourse and process of theory change in science: in Thomas Kuhn's (1962) account that draws on Wittgenstein's work, theory change is not a rational process. What he calls 'normal science' accumulates anomalies that eventually lead to revolutionary science and the overturning of the old paradigm. Historical philosophers of science like Kuhn, Paul Feyerabend, N. Russell Hanson, Michael Polanyi, Stephen Toulmin and Mary Hesse—all influenced by Wittgenstein—started questioning the rational reconstruction of scientific change offered by logical positivists that pictured science progressing in a rational and incremental way. Similarly, Gaston Bachelard, George Canguilhem, Louis Althusser and Michel Foucault in the tradition of French historical epistemology were investigating the question of change versus continuity in theory, *epistemes* and worldviews on the Continent. The notion of 'epistemological break' was first used by Bachelard and later by Althusser and Foucault to describe 'ruptures' or discontinuities in thought. Kuhn used the concept of 'paradigm shift'. The rupture might be the moment when science separated itself from its non-scientific past and the history of science, might thus be understood less as a process of discovery and more as the overcoming of an obstacle to knowledge, thought and belief based on the reorganization of the very possibility of knowledge.

One lesson we might take from Wittgenstein in retrospect is that social and cultural processes are involved in the change of forms of life that change historically very slowly, a process that Wittgenstein likens to a shifting riverbed. Even if one takes a cognitive orientation to worldview—that is to consider worldviews as loose networks of beliefs that hang together that can be articulated and recognized—it is difficult to envisage the process of change and what it involves. If our worldview is the way we make sense of the world and our place in the world, then any change that threatens our worldview also threatens our existence. This surely is at once a philosophical and pedagogical problem that is paramount when earlier organic forms of life mesh and intermingle, and come into conflict. If worldviews are also embedded in forms of life and are part of the language, speaking, gestures and cultural engagements to what extent are they open to articulation as a system—to what extent are they open to change. This question is relevant to the questioning of specific practices such a genital mutilation of girls or infanticide—the question of the practice might raise a basic question for aspects of the worldview (in this case the role and status of women). To what extent do worldviews operate at the conscious level and how accessible are they to discussion and analysis? To what extent do they imply incommensurability or linguistic and cultural relativity? On these, and related matters Wittgenstein is very influenced by the German tradition of *Weltanschuung.*

Wittgenstein wanted to liberate us from a view of modern philosophy as foundational (certain and accurate representations), but he did not want offer another metaphysics to then replace the Cartesian worldview. Wittgenstein sidesteps Descartes' epistemology and metaphysics by moving to language and philosophical grammar to talk of a non-Cartesian worldview (*Weltbild*) consisting of unverifiable *forms of life* and non-representational language. Thus, Wittgenstein introduces a new way of thinking in order to change our *way of seeing*. This is a particular understanding of *Weltanschuung* (worldview) and *Weltbild* that Wittgenstein was interested in shifting our modern conception of the world. His aim 'To shew the fly the way out of the fly-bottle' (PI §310) could not be pursued by the methods of modern philosophy based on logic and forms of argumentation. In *On Certainty*, Wittgenstein turns to a meta-consideration of world-pictures where his pluralism consist in epistemically unjustified *forms of life* and language-games within which people construct their worldviews. A *Weltbild* is not chosen but rather culturally inherited and it functions like a governing mythology—basically different conceptual schema, frameworks, or paradigms—which require understanding in terms of *pictures* (Naugle 2002), that is in aesthetic terms closer to art than philosophy.

### 4.4.2 *Weltanschuung*

In *Worldview: The History of a Concept* Naugle (2002), the neo-Calvinist documents the use of the term and philological history of the term *Weltanschuung*. To summarize Naugle, the term *Weltanschuung* or worldview is first coined by Kant (c. 1790) in the *Critique of Judgement* (Naugle 2002, 58 fn) where it is used to mean the sense perception of the world or world given to the senses. The notion was picked up by philosophers in the tradition of German idealism, particularly, Fichte and Schelling who interpreted it as understanding the universe of beings (as the purpose of philosophy). For Schelling, it is a product of the unconscious intellect and subterranean impressions and he stamps it with the meaning of an intellectual, rather than sensory perception, of the cosmos. Then it becomes rooted in use by

Hegel, Schegel, Novalis, Schieliermacher and Goethe—by poets and philosophers —and enormously popular in the nineteenth century (Naugle 2002, 61).

The concept migrates to the English-speaking world being first used by William James in 1868. The Oxford dictionary views it as a loan word comprised of *Welt* (world) and *Anschauung* (perception), naturalized as 'worldview' and ignored by philosophy or given little attention. In the nineteenth century at the hands of Hegel, Kierkegaard and Dilthey, it becomes the framework within which to grasp the meaning of life. Worldviews are 'rooted in the contingencies of human and historical experience', reflecting the structure of the human soul and as such become expressions of religious and poetic perspectives. Nietzsche used the word often and in the breakdown of idealism following his naturalistic and historicist leanings he came to talk of worldviews as both homogeneous and consistent set of values, allowing him to differentiate Hellenistic, Dionysian, Christian, Hegelian and mechanistic views of life (Naugle 2002, 100).

### *4.4.3 Wittgenstein on* **Weltanschuung***: The Influence of Spengler*

There is no doubt that Wittgenstein was influenced by Oswald Spengler and especially his conception of history and his method developed in *The Decline of the West* (1991)—*Der Untergang des Abendlandes*—published as two volumes in 1918 and 1923 respectively. Wittgenstein acknowledges the importance of Spengler's thinking on his own in a number of comments in the early 1940s (Wittgenstein 1999, NW 125 31v 1 Apr, 1942). Earlier in 1930 he suggests that while there is much that is 'irresponsible in specifics' there are also 'many genuinely significant thoughts' that touch on what he himself has thought: 'The possibility of several self-contained systems which, once one has them, look as though one were a continuation of the other. And all of this also connects with the thought that we really don't know (or consider) how much can be taken from or given to humans' (Wittgenstein 1999, NW 183 17 6 May, 1930, cited in Cahill 2006).

In the draft Preface to the unpublished *Philosophical Remarks* Wittgenstein writes:

> This book is written for those who are in sympathy with the spirit in which it is written. This is not, I believe, the spirit of the main current of European and American civilization. This spirit of this civilization makes itself manifest in the industry, architecture and music of our time, in its fascism and socialism, and it is alien and uncongenial to the author…. I have no sympathy for the current of European civilization and do not understand it goals if it has any…. Our civilization is characterised by the word 'progress.' Progress is its form rather than making progress being one of its features. Typically, it constructs. It is occupied with building an ever more complicated structure… I am not interested in constructing a building, so much as having a perspicuous view of the foundations of possible buildings. (CV, 6–7)

Wittgenstein takes the motto of the *Philosophical Investigations* from a line in Johann Nestroy's play *Der Schiltzling* (*The Protégé*): 'Anyway, the thing about progress is that it always seems greater than it really is' (see Cahill 2006, 71). What Wittgenstein is drawing attention to is the attitude that characterizes the West's worldview of progress. What he takes from Nestroy and Spengler is how technical or technological progress does not change or represent *moral* progress—and how little moral progress, if any, has been achieved.

The influence of Oswald Spengler in terms of method which Haller (1988, 79) characterizes as that of a 'Gestalt analysis of history' or the 'method of descriptive morphology'. Spengler's bestselling *The Decline of the West* becomes a critical point of discussion in philosophy of history in the interwar period projecting an allegedly scientific thesis about the rise and decline of culture—the so-called 'morphology of history' that views cultures as living organic entities. This organic conception of history reflects certain racial, biological and genetic paradigms, after Mendel and Darwin, popular in these years to explain the patterns of life and social decay.

Wittgenstein's '*forms of life*' draw on such an organic conception and the concept of a 'perspicuous presentation' (*übersichtliche Darstellung*) is of fundamental philosophical significance as a means of coping with what he calls the 'unsurveyability' (*Unübersichtlichkeit*) of 'our grammar' (PI §122; see Martin 2016).

> A main source of our failure to understand is that we do not command a clear view of the use of our words. – Our grammar is lacking in this sort of perspicuity. A perspicuous presentation produces just that understanding which consists in 'seeing connections'. Hence the importance of finding and inventing intermediate cases. The concept of a perspicuous presentation is of fundamental significance for us. It earmarks the form of account we give, the way we look at things. (A kind of "*Weltanschuung*" that seems typical of our time. Spengler.) (PI §122; cf. RFGB, in PO 133)

Perspicuous presentations provide a set of internal connections between the elements that make up a form of life—not only expressions but also gestures and pictures—but all aspects of meaningful human activity.

### 4.4.4 On Certainty

Naugle argues that there are four basic elements in Wittgenstein's discussion of world-picture in *On Certainty*:

> First, a *Weltbild* forms one's way of seeing and conceiving of the world and its basic character. Second, a *Weltbild* is not chosen as a result of some verification process, but rather is inherited from one's content and so serves as the assumed substratum for all thinking, acting, judging, and living. Third, the narratives constituting a world picture function as a kind of governing mythology. Finally, world pictures are promulgated rhetorically and are accepted in faith. Given these characteristics, world pictures and forms of life with their inherent language games seem almost identical.

Wittgenstein rejected *Weltanschuung* as a hangover from the Cartesian era preferring instead 'forms of life' that are rooted in life, language and meaning. As Naugle argues, world-pictures in Wittgensteinian terms are not to be conceived of as epistemically credible constructs competing for rational adherence, but as webs of belief as ways of organizing reality where 'framework facts' are the 'axis', 'river-bed', 'scaffolding', or 'hinges' of a particular way of thinking and acting. In *On Certainty*, Wittgenstein demonstrates that Moore's defence of common sense and proof of an external world is undertaken in a Cartesian framework. More broadly speaking, we might say that the question of *Weltanschuung* pertains to conceptual schemes and the problem of conceptual relativism that lies at the heart of Western philosophy. We have already briefly discussed Kuhn's 'paradigm', and might equally mention in this regard Davidson's 'conceptual schemes', Goodman's 'world version', Korners' 'categorical framework', Carnap's 'linguistic framework', Marx's and Mannheim's 'ideology' (Naugle 2002).

In an age of globalization and inter-culturalism where the 'experiment' of openness increasingly creates a communicational and informational interconnectedness developed through the Internet 3.0 and a range of new social media tools based on apps and mobile technologies, the question of the conflict and interactivity of worldviews and forms of life become a dominant philosophical and pedagogical problem. How do we escape the 'picture that holds us captive'? How do we teach others to question and escape the picture that holds them captive?

### *4.4.5 Escaping Enthrallment in Pictures*

> If we imagine the facts otherwise than as they are, certain language-games lose some of their importance, while others become important. And in this way there is an alteration – a gradual one – in the use of the vocabulary of a language. (OC §63)
>
> When language-games change, then there is a change in concepts, and with the concepts the meanings of words change. (OC §65)

To think differently, as in no longer holding certain hinge propositions or world-pictures to be indubitable (OC §248; PI §104), entails shifts in the bedrock or riverbanks that channel thoughts. Such gradual shifts allow for the emergence of new world-pictures.

> But what men consider reasonable or unreasonable alters. At certain periods men find reasonable what at other periods they found unreasonable. And vice versa.
>
> But is there no objective character here?
>
> *Very* intelligent and well-educated people believe in the story of creation in the Bible, while others hold it is proven false, and the grounds of the latter are well known to the former. (OC §336)

As David Owen explains, to escape an 'enthralling' picture embedded in our language we need to undergo a genealogical process of self-overcoming. The genealogical nature of this post-foundational approach to critique has its origin in Nietzsche's *Genealogy of Morals*, and the concept of *resentiment* or 'revaluation of values' (cf. Bearn 1997). We may readily see this influence in Foucault's work (e.g., a genealogy of the *carceral* in *Discipline and Punish*). We can also detect its subtle presence in Wittgenstein's presentation of the way 'an entire mythology is laid down in our language' (Phil., p. 199; RFGB, p. 133) and how such a mythology can ensnare us. In Nietzschean language, Wittgenstein describes breaking with the herd as initially destructive work: or a process of self-liberation through a different kind of exertion (see PO 185 in Ch 2). The solution is to attend to language in use, instead of building elaborate theories: 'What we do is bring words back from their metaphysical to their ordinary use' (PI §116). The philosophical question, for Wittgenstein, is how we might escape from captivating pictures by resisting 'the bewitchment of the intelligence by means of language' (PI §109).

In less metaphorical terms, Owen (2003) and Tully (2003) identify steps taken in this self-transformative process. Owen offers a set of characteristics that are shared by Nietzsche and Foucault's genealogical critique. Owen summarizes the stages in this process as follows:

> a. It identifies a picture that holds us captive, whereby this captivity obstructs our capacity to make sense of ourselves as agents in ways that matter to us;
> b. This account involves a redescription of this picture that contrasts it with another way of seeing the issue in order to free us from captivity to this picture;
> c. It provides an account of how we have become held captive by this picture, which enables us to make sense of ourselves as agents and, more particularly, to make sense of how we have failed to make sense of ourselves in ways that matter to us;
> d. Insofar as this account engages with our cares and commitments, it motivates us to engage in the practical working out of this redescription of ourselves as agents.
>
> (Owen 2003, 95; cf. Tully 2002, 2003. The four-stage process Owen elaborates (the idea of giving a redescription) is more fully explained here by Tully, as Owen acknowledges.)

Owen uses *On Certainty* quotes in which Wittgenstein shows how *world-pictures* (*weltbilds* such as the earth's sphericity) are embedded in our language and form an otherwise 'groundless basis' for our unreflective action (OC §94–5, 146–7, 162 and 262).

> It may be for example that *all enquiry on our part* is set so as to exempt certain propositions from doubt, if they are ever formulated. They lie apart from the route travelled by enquiry. (OC §88)
>
> And now if I were to say 'It is my unshakeable conviction that etc.', this means in the present case too that I have not consciously arrived at the conviction by following a particular line of thought, but that it is anchored in all my *questions and answers*, so anchored that I cannot touch it. (OC §103)

> Now it gives our way of looking at things, and our researches, their form. Perhaps it was once disputed. But perhaps for unthinkable ages, it has belonged to the *scaffolding* of our thoughts. (Every human being has parent.) (OC§ 211)

To this genealogy of our bedrock, he applies Wittgenstein's concept of *continuous seeing of an aspect*, contributing jointly to critical perspectives on what he calls *aspectival captivity* (Owen 2003, 92). Owen distinguishes the concept of *aspectival captivity* from ideological entrapment (or 'false consciousness'), in that in the former concept it is not concerned with 'truth' itself, but with how we determine, play or produce the *true-and-false*. In the latter case, those held captive by false beliefs may be liberated through ideology-critique (e.g. elucidation of internal contradictions or factual errors). He elaborates:

> The state of unfreedom described by the concept of *aspectival captivity* is... logically distinct from that described by the concept of ideological captivity, most notably in that *aspectival captivity* is independent of the truth or falsity of the beliefs held by the agent. Hence, too, the kind of practice of criticism required to address this condition of unfreedom – namely genealogy – is also logically distinct in kind from ideology-critique. ...In so far as *apectival captivity* is characterized by agents' reflecting and acting on themselves as subjects in terms of a given picture as the *only* possible picture open to them, the initial aim of genealogy is to enable them to free themselves from *aspectival captivity* by exhibiting the possibility of other pictures. (Owen 2003, 92)

Owen explains that *aspectival captivity* is self-imposed constraint grounded in our contingent practices, as persons under the captivating hold of a picture do not allow themselves to reflect more critically on alternative pictures. He explains further that there is no logical space for such a person to entertain false second-order beliefs about the range of first-order beliefs open to him. It is not a matter of having a false picture of the world, which ideology-critique can expose or debunk (e.g. the work of the Frankfurt school); it is more that a deeply rooted or ingrained *world-picture* does not allow for alternative pictures and, hence, an unfreedom due to fixating on too narrow a range of potential aspects.

> The point can be put this way: it is a necessary condition of the agent's having such a false second-order belief that the agent recognizes the possibility of such second-order belief being true or false, but to be held captive by a picture or perspective is just to fail to recognize this possibility as a possibility. (Owen 2003, 90)

By way of example, Owen (2003, 83) notes Wittgenstein's opposition to the picture (embedded, for instance, in Kant's *Pedagogy*) of the progressive stages of social evolution (critiqued by Wittgenstein in *Remarks on Fraser's Golden Bough*).[14] Referring to the deeply ingrained picture of the awakening of consciousness in higher animals and 'man' (traditionally depicted as a kind of epiphany

[14]See Kant's stages theory in relation to education, in the *Pedagogy* (Kant 1904, section 1–12).

Tully also refers to the Kantian 'stages of progress' theory as being sedimented in our worldview, in an unpublished paper: The Persistence of Empire: A legacy of colonialism and decolonisation (The Panel on After Colonialism. *The Conference on Colonialism and its Legacies, The Annual Conference for the Study of Political Thought*, University of Chicago, April 22–25, 2004).

for these beings), Wittgenstein offers a remark that illustrates the need for such genealogical work:

> What this language primarily describes is a picture. What is to be done with the picture, how it is to be used, is still obscure. Quite clearly, however, it must be explored if we want to understand the sense of what we are saying. But the picture seems to spare us this work: it already points to a particular use. This is how it takes us in. (PI, p. 184)

Drawing on David Owen and James Tully, Temilini (2015)[15] sought to free us from the captivating picture that Wittgenstein somehow endorses a conservative view, resulting from overemphasis or misreading of training cases. The 'primacy of the training reading', he argues, goes hand in hand with two kinds of sceptical arguments around contextualism and incommensuarability, creating a worrisome 'orthodoxy around training and initiation' (Temilini 2015, 66–7). Most productively in this regard, after Tully, Temilini points to an opening in the rule-following argument where Wittgenstein addresses not only how pupils are trained into conventionally following rules *as others do*, but where the seasoned educator also recognizes cases where pupils reasonably deviate from anticipated rules: 'Going *against* the rule in actual cases' (PI §201; see above in connection with rule-drift). The paradox (see Kripke 1982) of who determines what is right-or-wrong here focuses attention on the destabilizing moment of indeterminacy, potentially inaugurating freedoms within the rules (see Zerilli 2005, 139, 146).

> Tully is actually making more than argument here. The first is that being guided and trained is not something 'mechanical' or 'reducible to the behaviourist's causal compulsion of habit'. Citing PI, s. 172, he agues instead that there are many different ways we can be inducted into language-games that don't involve habit and that are not tantamount to behavioural conditioning. On the contrary, as Wittgenstein says, 'being guided is a particular experience'. So being trained to follow a rule doesn't somehow turn off our critical or rational faculties. We're not just trapped in an uncritically determined set of norms and practices, because we do have such critical abilities to 'go on differently'. In contrast to the argument suggested by the pedagogical reading, Tully argues that it's not just 'seasoned practitioners' who are capable of going on differently. 'Novitiates', too, are able to question and raise doubts. This argument implies that training is a family resemblance concept and that being initiated and inducted into a form of life does not necessarily entail either strong or weak forms of conventionalism. Training does not entail either the determinacy or the primacy of context. It does not imprison us in our way of life or destroy any possibility of liberating ourselves from convention. (Temilini 2015, 173)[16]

With Temilini, we too renounce the conservative reading of Wittgenstein. Within philosophy of education, however, there is a widely shared and well-established view that eschews the conservative reading of Wittgenstein without at the same time forfeiting his deep connections to education (see Stickney

---

[15]Temilini (2015) is the publication of his doctoral dissertation, supervised by James Tully. Tully was also Stickney's advisor, and we appreciate his help in directing us to Michael Temilini, who kindly contributed at a chapter on Tully's use of Wittgenstein and the presentation of cases in political philosophy (see Temilini 2017).

[16]Temelini refers readers to PI 5, 6, 7, 9, 27, 86, 137, 143, 144, 145, 146, 156, 157, 162, 185, 189, 235, 362, 630, pp. 191, 200.

2005; Burbules 2005; Smeyers 2017; Standish 2017; Gasparatou 2017). We hope to have moved past the negative reading of training cases through our exposition of Wittgenstein's remarks on teaching and learning in previous chapters (see especially Ch 2 and 3), as well as our discussion of their role in his later methodology (see above, re: PI §122). It is an educator aware of alternate 'pictures' that Wittgenstein addresses the negative consequences of some conventional, dogmatic views (see CV 28e). Entrenchment in 'world-pictures' causes us to feel 'intellectually very distant' from those who think differently (OC §108), much as the locals in the Austrian villages, where Wittgenstein taught elementary school found him to be 'strange' (*Fremd*) and he considered them to be narrow-minded (Monk 1990, 194–197, 209 and 233). His 'Lecture on Aesthetics' is an example of where he attempts to revise our way of thinking about the subject:

> Much of what we are doing is trying to change the style of thinking. (LC 28)

As a practicing teacher and philosopher, he is equally aware that it is often difficult to provide sufficient grounds or reasons for changing the way people customarily think and act. Although the philosopher may offer a perspicuous description of enthralling traps in language (PI §§109 and 122), Wittgenstein was sceptical about the philosopher's (messianic) ability to extricate people from these traps.[17] Recall his motto, drawn from Nestroy, on how progress rarely measures up to our expectations.

> A philosopher says "Look at things like this!" – but in the first place doesn't ensure that people will look at things like that, and in the second place his admonitions may come altogether too late; it's possible, moreover, that such an admonition can achieve nothing in any case and that the impetus for such a change in the way things are perceived has to originate somewhere else entirely. For instance it is by no means clear whether Bacon started anything moving, other than the surface of his reader's minds. Nothing seems to me less likely than that a scientist or mathematician who reads me should be seriously influenced in the way he works.... I ought never to hope for more than indirect influence. (CV 61–62)

Wittgenstein repeatedly emphasized that only a change in practice could bring about a new way of thinking in society, much as a new mode of transportation could alter the sickness of an age dependent on the personal automobile (RFM II.4).

> In philosophizing we may not *terminate* a disease of thought. It must run its natural course, and *slow* cure is all important. (That is why mathematicians are such bad philosophers.) (Z §382)

Although social change is often slow, due to language-games crystallizing into our common *bedrock*, it also results in the conservation of practices and traditions that inform our cultural identities. One remarking that humans are 'ceremonial animals'

[17]You have a new conception and interpret it as seeing a new object. You interpret a grammatical movement made by yourself as a quasi-physical phenomenon which you are observing. ...What you primarily discovered was a new way of looking at things. (OC §401)

(RFGB in PO 129),[18] Wittgenstein was also respectful of diverse ways of living, himself something of an outcast or recluse who could adopt a view from the margins (see Medina 2006). He was repulsed by Frazer's condescending view toward so-called 'primitive' peoples, noting how our 'kinship with those savages' shows in that our own language still has words for spiritual phenomena like 'ghosts' (RFGB, in PO 133) as well as rituals that may appear silly to outsiders.

> It is perfectly possible that we should be inclined to call people who behaved like this insane. And yet we don't call everyone insane who acts similarly within the forms of our culture, who uses words 'without purpose'. (Think of the coronation of a King.) (RFM, I.152)

Wittgenstein created scenes of imaginary woodcutters using seemingly incomprehensible selling practices (by area instead of volume or weight, or even by effort or need, RFM I.146–151), or people using worn coins with no apparent value (RFM: I.151–2), to demonstrate that meaningful usage hinges off training into a *consensus of action*.

> One of the most important methods I use is to imagine a historical development for our ideas different from what actually occurred. If we do this, we see the problem from a completely new angle. (CV 37e)

Wittgenstein educates by describing alternate ways of life so as to show us by example how people can learn to believe very different worldviews and act with certainty in ways that often vary from our own. This ethological approach gives us a heightened appreciation of our solidarity within a *form of life*, but also the promise of revising one through further education.

> "We are sure of it" does not just mean that every single person is certain of it, but that we belong to a community which is bound together by science and education. (OC §298)

> I want to say: an education quite different from ours might also be the foundation of quite different concepts. For here life would run on differently. (Z §387–88; cf. PI, p. 230)

## References

Aerts, D., Apostel, L., De Moor, B., Hellemans, S., Maex, E., Van Belle, H., et al. (2007). *World views: From fragmentation to integration.* Internet Edition 2007. Originally published in 1994 by VUB Press: Brussels Internet edition by Clément Vidal and Alexander Riegler. http://www.vub.ac.be/CLEA/pub/books/worldviews.pdf.

Bearn, G. (1997). *Waking to wonder: Wittgenstein's existential investigations.* Albany, NY: Stature University of New York Press.

Bowell, T. (2017). Wittgenstein on teaching and learning the rules: Taking him at his word. In M. A. Peters & J. Stickney (Eds.), *A companion to Wittgenstein on education: Pedagogical investigations* (pp. 643–658). Singapore: Springer.

Burbules, N. (2005). Learning and the limits of doubt. Response paper to Jeff Stickney. In K. Howe (Ed.), *Philosophy of Education Society Yearbook* (pp. 308–310). Paper given at the PES annual meeting, San Francisco.

---

[18]Of his own remark, he says (PO 129): 'That is, no doubt, partly wrong and nonsensical, but there is also something right about it'.

Burbules, N. (2008). Tacit teaching. *Educational Philosophy and Theory, 40*(5), 666–677.
Cahill, K. (2006). The concept of progress in Wittgenstein thought. *The Review of Metaphysics, 60* (September), 71–100.
Cahill, K. M. (n.d.). *Wittgenstein and Spengler.* http://wab.uib.no/agora/tools/alws/collection-1-issue-1-article-71.annotate.
Cavell, S. (1979). *The claim of reason: Wittgenstein, skepticism, morality, and tragedy.* Oxford: Oxford University Press.
Gasparatou, R. (2017). On "the temptation to attack common sense". In M. A. Peters & J. Stickney (Eds.), *A companion to Wittgenstein on education: Pedagogical investigations* (pp. 275–286). Singapore: Springer.
Green, T. (1968). Topology of the teaching concept. In C. J. B. MacMillan & T. W. Nelson (Eds.), *Concepts of teaching.* New York: Rand McNally.
Haller, R. (1988). *Questions on Wittgenstein.* Lincoln: University of Nebraska Press.
Hirst, P. (1971). What is teaching? *Journal of Curriculum Studies, 3*(1), 5–18.
Hirst, P., & Peters, R. S. (1970). *The logic of education.* London: Routledge and Kegan Paul.
Hunter, J. F. M. (1973). Telling. In *Essays after Wittgenstein.* Toronto and Buffalo: University of Toronto Press.
Hunter, J. F. M. (1985). The harried mathematics instructor. In Understanding Wittgenstein (Ed.), *Studies of philosophical investigations.* Glasgow: Edinburgh University Press.
Johansson, V. (2017). The weight of dogmatism: Investigating "learning" in Dewey's pragmatism and Wittgenstein's ordinary language philosophy. In M. A. Peters & J. Stickney (Eds.), *A companion to Wittgenstein on education: Pedagogical investigations* (pp. 339–352). Singapore: Springer.
Kant, I. (1904). In E. F. Buchner (Ed. & Trans.), *The educational theory of Immanuel Kant.* Philadelphia: J.B. Lippincott.
Kern, A. (2004). Understanding scepticism: Wittgenstein's paradoxical reinterpretation of sceptical doubt. In D. McManus (Ed.), *Wittgenstein and scepticism.* New York: Routledge.
Komisar, P. (1968). Teaching: Act and enterprise. In C. J. B. MacMillan & T. W. Nelson (Eds.), *Concepts of teaching.* New York: Rand McNally.
Kripke, S. (1982). The Wittgensteinian paradox. In *Wittgenstein on rules and private language. An elementary exposition.* Oxford: Basil Blackwell.
Kuhn, T. (1962). *The Structure of Scientific Revolutions* (3rd ed.). Chicago and London:University of Chicago Press. (Reprinted 1999).
Martin, C. G. (2016). Wittgenstein on perspicuous presentations and grammatical self-knowledge. *Nordic Wittgenstein Review, 5*(1), 79–106.
McDowell, J. (1998). Wittgenstein on following a rule. In *Mind, value, and reality.* Cambridge, MA: Cambridge University Press.
Medina, J. (2002). *The unity of Wittgenstein's philosophy. Necessity, intelligibility, and normativity.* Albany: State University of New York Press.
Medina, J. (2006). *Speaking from elsewhere. A new contextualist perspective on meaning, identity, and discursive agency.* Albany: State University of New York Press.
Monk, R. (1990). *Ludwig Wittgenstein: The duty of genius.* London: Cape.
Naugle, D. (2002). *Worldview: The history of a concept.* Grand Rapids, MI: Wm. B. Eerdmans Publishing Company.
Owen, D. (2003). Genealogy as perspicuous representation. In C. Heyes (ed.), *The grammar of politics. Wittgenstein and political philosophy* (pp. 82–98). Ithaca, NY: Cornell University Press.
Peters, M. A., & Stickney, J. (2018, in press). Philosophy of education 1945-2010 and the 'education of reason': Post-foundational approaches through Dewey, Wittgenstein, and Foucault. In K. Becker & I. Thomson (Eds.), *The Cambridge history of philosophy, 1945-2015.* Cambridge: Cambridge University Press.
Peters, M. A., Burbules, N., & Smeyers, P. (2008). *Saying and Doing: Wittgenstein as a Pedagogical Philosopher.* Boulder: Paradigm Press.
Searle, J. (1995). *The construction of social reality.* New York: The Free Press.

Smeyers, P. (2017). "This is simply what I do." On the relevance of Wittgenstein's alleged conservatism and the debate about Cavell's legacy for children and grown-ups. In M. A. Peters & J. Stickney (Eds.), *A companion to Wittgenstein on education: Pedagogical investigations* (pp. 241–259). Singapore: Springer.

Spengler, O. (1991). *The decline of the west* (A. Helps & H. Werner, Eds.; C. F. Atkinson, Trans.). New York: Oxford University Press.

Standish, P. (2017). This is simply what I do too: A response to Paul Smeyers. In M. A. Peters & J. Stickney (Eds.), *A companion to Wittgenstein on education: Pedagogical investigations* (pp. 261–274). Singapore: Springer.

Stickney, J. (2005). Teaching and learning in Wittgenstein's philosophic method. In K. Howe (Ed.), *Philosophy of Education Society yearbook, 2005* (pp. 299–308). Paper given at the PES annual meeting, San Francisco. http://ojs.ed.uiuc.edu/index.php/pes/article/viewFile/1637/371.

Stickney, J. (2009). Wittgenstein's contextualist approach to judging 'sound' teaching: Escaping enthrallment in criteria-based assessments. *Educational Theory, 59*(2), (June) 197–216. N. Burbules (Ed.).

Stickney, J. (2014). Wittgenstein for adolescents? Post-foundational epistemology in high school philosophy. *Ethics and Education, 9*(2), 201–219.

Stickney, J., Anderson, S., Jopling, D., Martyr-Andre, J., Oja, L., Quejada, E., et al. (2011). *Philosophy. Thinkers, theories & questions*. Toronto: McGraw-Hill Ryerson.

Stickney, J., & Peters, M. A. (2017). Journeys with Wittgenstein: Assembling sketches of a philosophical landscape. In M. A. Peters & J. Stickney (Eds.), *A companion to Wittgenstein on education: Pedagogical investigations* (pp. 3–28). Singapore: Springer.

Taylor, C. (1995). Overcoming epistemology. In *Philosophical arguments*. Cambridge, MA and London: Harvard University Press.

Temelini, M. (2015). The ability to go on differently: The diversity of being trained and guided; and, The primacy of training in a shared form of life. In *Wittgenstein and the study of politics*. Toronto: University of Toronto Press.

Temilini, M. (2017). Learning politics by means of examples. In M. A. Peters & J. Stickney (Eds.), *A companion to Wittgenstein on education: Pedagogical investigations* (pp. 287–304). Singapore: Springer.

Tully, J. (2002). Political philosophy as a critical activity. *Political Theory, 30*(4), 533–555.

Tully, J. (2003). Wittgenstein and political philosophy. Understanding practices of critical reflection. In C. Heyes (Ed.), *The grammar of politics. Wittgenstein and political philosophy* (pp. 17–42). Ithaca and London: Cornell University Press. [Originally, *Political Theory*, (1989) 17(2): 172–204.].

Wittgenstein, L. (1956). *Remarks on the foundation of mathematics* (G. E. M. Anscombe, Trans.). Oxford: Basil Blackwell (RFM).

Wittgenstein, L. (1961). *Tractatus logico-philosophicus* (D. F. Pears & B. F. McGuinness, Trans.). London: Routledge and Kegan Paul (TLP).

Wittgenstein, L. (1967). *Zettel* (G. E. M. Anscombe, Trans.). Oxford: Basil Black-well (Z).

Wittgenstein, L. (1968). *Philosophical investigations* (3rd ed., G. E. M. Anscombe, Trans.). Oxford: Basil Blackwell (PI§, or PI, pg.).

Wittgenstein, L. (1969). *On certainty* (D. Paul & G. E. M. Anscombe, Trans.). Oxford: Basil Blackwell (OC).

Wittgenstein, L. (1980). *Culture and value* (G. H. von Wright, Ed., in collaboration with H. Nyman, P. Winch, Trans.). Oxford: Basil Blackwell (CV).

Wittgenstein, L. (1982). *Last writings on the philosophy of psychology: Vol. 1. Preliminary studies for part II of "Philosophical investigations"* (G. H. von Wright & H. Nyman Eds., C. G. Lukhardt & M. A. E. Aue, Trans.). Oxford: Blackwell (LW I).

Wittgenstein, L. (1999). *Nachlass*. Bergen, Norway: Wittgensteinarkivet (NW).

Zerilli, L. (2005). *Feminism and the abyss of freedom*. Chicago, IL: University of Chicago Press.

29963262R00074

Printed in Great Britain
by Amazon